Taking the Guidon

Exceptional Leadership at the Company Level

Nate Allen and Tony Burgess

First Edition 2001

Editorial Staff: Pete Kilner, Janet Holliday, and Lisa Burgess-Noudehou

Formatting for publishing by Brace Barber

Cover art by Beverly Cooper

Published by the Center for Company-Level Leadership, Delaware.

Printed in the United States of America

ISBN 0-9678292-1-6

First Edition

"Taking the Guidon" Significance

The unit guidon serves to identify the unit, is a symbol of the commander's authority and presence, and represents the collective pride and spirit of all soldiers-past and present-who have served under it. Historically, the guidon accompanied the commander into battle where, in the heat and confusion of the close fight, it emboldened and rallied the soldiers to accomplish the mission.

Today, the unit guidon continues to be an honored symbol of the commander's authority and responsibility, and it connects the valorous deeds of past warriors with today's soldiers who continue the proud tradition of selfless service to our Nation.

An Army unit conducts a change-of-command ceremony whenever a new commander takes charge. The central rite of this ceremony is the passing of the unit guidon from the outgoing commander to the incoming commander. By taking the guidon, the new commander signals his or her selfless commitment to the traditions, values, and soldiers that the guidon represents.

Foreword

by Major General (Retired) John G. Meyer, Jr.
Author of *Company Command: The Bottom Line*

Taking the Guidon: Exceptional Leadership at the Company Level is an absolute must read for all young officers preparing for company command.

Nate Allen and Tony Burgess provide a tremendously valuable service to their fellow officers by succinctly, accurately, and passionately describing how to command an Army company effectively. They take the key essentials of leadership, discipline, fitness, and motivation and provide the reader with "tricks of the trade" that are invaluable for command not only at the company level but also at any level of command.

This work provides a new commander with all the tools to succeed. The authors start at the beginning, prior to command, by laying out all the research and preparation that should be done to ensure new commanders are ready on day one. The demands on young officers today generally preclude adequate and timely preparation; consequently, the authors' advice is solid.

The authors extensively cover leader development. They are right—it takes time and effort, and the results do not happen overnight. They provide very good practical examples on how to establish a viable leader development program. Particularly important is to always lead by example. In their words, "Your soldiers will care far more about what you say with your actions than your words."

The training, maintenance, and safety section is right on the money—particularly the part on training. Their practical coverage and very helpful hints on how to improve training and how to make training your company's priority may be the most beneficial part of this really excellent and useful book. They include maintenance in this section because maintenance is training. The coverage of physical training is one of the best I've seen. It is well thought out, easy to follow and implement, and filled with ideas that, if applied properly, will definitely increase the PT standards of soldiers.

They conclude by letting you know how to build a winning team and how to take care of soldiers with focus on the UCMJ, awards, family support groups, and the all-important BOSS program.

Bottom Line: Nate Allen and Tony Burgess, two very dedicated soldiers, care enough to make a positive difference for all company commanders. *"Taking the Guidon: Exceptional Leadership at the Company Level"* is not only a quick but also a valuable reference for all future young leaders. Keep it handy; you'll find yourself dipping back into it regularly, especially for the concrete and practical tips it provides. An added benefit, again their "brain child," is to keep this book and the command concepts they have collected from others alive on their Web site: http://www.companycommand.com. If you haven't read this book or used the Web site, you'll still be standing at the station while the train is miles down the track.

PS: If you don't know what DWYSYWD, DTRT and DSSS mean, you missed the train altogether.

Contents

Chapter 3 – Physically Fit

Chapter 4 – Motivated

Conclusion /   159

About CompanyCommand & PlatoonLeader /   161

Bibliography /   165

Preface

Combat is the ultimate team sport; the cost of losing is death. As an Army leader, your mission is to build a winning team of disciplined, fit, and motivated soldiers that will accomplish the mission. You and your team must approach this goal with the same intensity that the greatest football teams have approached preparing for the Super Bowl. Just as championship teams eat, sleep, breathe, and live their sport, so must combat units if they are to survive and accomplish their mission on the battlefield. Your greatest challenge is to create a culture in which your soldiers are focused and willing to pay the price it takes to be ready for combat. In this book, you will find some input to the age-old dialogue on how to create a team and harness its energy to accomplish uncommon results.

Leading soldiers is our inspiration; doing so has affected every part of our lives. To begin with, the knowledge that we would command a company motivated us to prepare doggedly for command. This book is a compilation of our research and thinking, validated by experience (both success and failure!). It is not meant to be prescriptive in nature; nor will all these ideas work for you and your situation. Rather, our intent is to spark your thinking and encourage you as you prepare for command.

We were fortunate to work with and watch some great leaders in action and to learn from some challenging experiences. Now we are in a position to pass on some of what we have learned. **Our desire is that reading this book motivates and challenges you while you prepare for and execute the most honorable mission in the world—leading American soldiers!**

Acknowledgments

First, we would like to thank our families. Our wives were an instrumental part of our command experiences and, without them, this book never would have been written. Nate thanks Joan, Ashley, Kristi, Dustin, and Ryan. Tony thanks Barbara, TJ, Jessie, and Jake.

We also thank the Army for giving us the opportunity to serve and lead soldiers.

There are many friends who gave us quality feedback and often-needed encouragement as our book emerged from the idea stage and grew into what it is now. We will mention a few here:

Pete Kilner was a major contributor to the writing of this book. He spent countless hours proofing our multiple drafts and suggesting better ways to communicate our message. Along the way he motivated and inspired us.

Janet Holliday and Lisa Maria Burgess-Noudehou also provided excellent editorial input—their feedback was especially helpful as we completed the book.

LTC Scott Snook provided mentorship and, in many ways, inspired us to put our ideas into action. He has especially influenced us in the area of leader development—Be, Know, Do!

LTG Lawson W. Magruder, III provided encouragement and valuable input to the content of the book. His positive response to our first draft version was a tremendous encouragement.

MG John G. Meyer, Jr. provided us the first practical book on company command when he wrote *Company Command: The Bottom Line.* His continued dedication to leadership at the company level is inspiring. His willingness to write the foreword to this book and to be involved with CompanyCommand.com is priceless.

Thanks to the members of the CompanyCommand.com Web site team who have sacrificed thousands of hours without remuneration simply because they believe in what we are doing. They are: Steve Schweitzer, Pete Kilner, Chris Engen, Steve Delvaux, Tom Woodie, Mark Tribus, Jeb Downing, Janet Holliday, and Craig Whiteside.

Brace Barber, author of *Ranger School: No Excuse Leadership,* took our book from the computer-disc stage to the final-book stage. His encouragement and expertise were instrumental in getting the book completed, and we owe him a debt of gratitude.

Finally, we would like to thank the soldiers with whom we have served. Anything that we have done or hope to do was and is possible because of you. Nate thanks the incredible soldiers of A/2-5 IN, "Quickstrike", 1SGs Wood, Coop and Torre, and lieutenants Villanueva, Kirby, Price, Tarlavsky, Miani, Fick, Ellis, and Duaine. Tony would like to thank 1SGs Neil, Uncangco, Hibbs, and Schott, and lieutenants Risdon, Wagh, Davis, Garcia, Wight, Denny, Gualtieri, Holt, and Bachelor.

This book is dedicated to company-level
leaders serving and leading soldiers
at the tip of the spear.

Captains—the leaders of companies, batteries, troops—fight. Captains and their officers, both commissioned and noncommissioned, work to insure that *soldiers* fight with skill, will, and teamwork. Captains, lieutenants, sergeants, and soldiers—the small units and their leaders—are the ones who fight. That's who's at the cutting edge. That's who delivers upon the enemy the combat power that the upper levels have put together.

– Colonel (Retired) Dandridge Malone[1]

So, let me tell you my opinion of training at the battalion level and below. This is where I see the heart of warfighting readiness. Yes, I know we've got brigade exercises. Divisions do BCTPs and corps do battle command training program exercises. But unless squads and platoons and companies can do what they need to do—which is what I call short-sword warfighting—unless you can get the short-sword warfighting business done, you're not ready.

–General Eric K. Shinseki[2]

---

[1] Dandridge M. Malone. *Small Unit Leadership: A Commonsense Approach*, 1983: p. 26.

[2] Remarks of Eric K. Shinseki, Chief of Staff, Army to the sergeants major luncheon, Association of the United States Army (AUSA), 16 October 2000.

CHAPTER 1 -- LEADERSHIP

Section 1. Learning – Prior To and During Command

> You will always be what you have always been, if
> you always do what you have always done.

Company command is a phenomenal leadership experience. Commanding 120+ soldiers — potentially in combat — is a responsibility that is quite humbling if you stop to think about it. It is an extremely challenging, sometimes lonely experience that will test your mettle, give you incredible satisfaction, and push you beyond your abilities. You will pour your soul into it and, in the end, you will join the thousands who remember it as the most professionally rewarding experience of their lives.

You may have seen how companies often take on the personalities of their commanders. Some have said that an organization is a shadow of its leader; it takes a "big" leader to cast a big shadow. Because the company commander has so much power and responsibility, he or she can easily become a "lid" on the company's level of effectiveness.[1]

While a lot of leadership springs from innate ability, character, and personality, there is a large element of leadership supported by skill and knowledge. It is important to be aware that there is a significant jump in leadership complexity from platoon leading to company commanding. The skill and knowledge that worked for you at the platoon level will not necessarily work at the company level.

Learning will not just happen—you must be committed to developing yourself as you prepare for command, and also *while* you command. The time to start preparing for company command is right now. If you are satisfied with yourself as you are, we feel confident in saying that you won't be the commander that you could be.

---

[1] John Maxwell calls this the "Law of the Lid: leadership ability determines a person's level of effectiveness." John Maxwell. *The 21 Most Powerful Minutes in a Leader's Day,* 2000: p. 1.

1

In this section, we will give you a few practical ideas that will help you better prepare for and command your unit. You can do three concrete things to increase your effectiveness. These are: writing down ideas for future use, committing yourself to read about leadership, and taking advantage of other commanders' experiences. Think of these techniques as learning combat multipliers that will "lift the lid" of your leadership capacity.

Write Your Ideas Down (Leader Notebook)

Start a "command idea" section in your leader notebook. In this section include ideas that you think of, see in action, or hear about that you might want to use while in command. Most good ideas disappear into the ether of lost thoughts unless you get them down on paper. One thought written down will later lead you to another thought that you never would have discovered without the first. In other words, reflecting upon previous thoughts often opens the door to other ideas. The implied task is that you actually review your notes and don't get caught up in the "tyranny of the urgent" as you take command, forgetting that your notes ever existed.

Our own notebooks are filled with ideas from our time as lieutenants, notes taken during OPDs, and our company command brainstorming sessions during the Captains' Career Course. These notes proved invaluable as we prepared for and commanded our companies. Many of the things we captured in our notebooks have ended up on the pages of this book.

Read (Professional Reading)

We hear a lot about professional reading being important to your development as an officer; it is even more critical to your preparation for command. Read as much as you possibly can on leadership, and take notes while you read. Bottom line: Whether or not you like reading, doing it is essential to both your preparation for command and your continued learning while in command. Taking notes while you read will ensure the knowledge you gain is not lost once you finish the book.[2] A fantastic resource for professional reading is the "Cmd Reading" section of the CompanyCommand.com Web site. The section offers ideas on developing a professional reading program for your subordinates, several recommended reading lists, links to on-line journals, book reviews, and comments from officers on how certain books impacted their ability to lead effectively.

Seek Advice and Counsel

It is crucial to take advantage of the experience of others. Why go into command on your experiences alone when you can go in with the collective experiences of many? On the top of your list will be your fellow commanders, your Battalion Commander, XO, S3, and CSM. Most importantly, seek out the outgoing commanders who probably know more about company command in your division than anyone else. Officers who depart command typically head off within days to some post-command assignment without ever sharing their experiences with up-and-coming commanders. This is a crime! Seek them out. We found that they will talk your ear off about the things that really excited them during command. Take a departing commander out to lunch a couple of times and "grill him" on leadership ideas. Let him know what the lunch will be about so he can think about it beforehand. Those coming out of command or other leadership positions love to talk about their experiences, are eager to share their ideas, and will often give you practical tools to use. Ask insightful questions like:

- What training really paid big dividends?
- What techniques helped you personally to be effective in the field?
- What is one thing you implemented that made a difference?

---

[2] Publishing your notes for your lieutenants is a great complement to your OPD program. They will not only learn from your notes, but they will learn how you think; additionally, they will be inspired by your reading example.

- If you could have focused more on one area, what would it have been?
- What really motivated the unit and helped build a winning team?
- How did you incorporate a combined arms focus in your training?

Seeking counsel is a way to learn things that you can apply right away that you might never have thought of or might not have figured out until much later on in your command.

Additionally, while you are in command, there is usually another commander doing something smarter, better, or more effectively than you. Don't let pride keep you from borrowing great ideas. Be a team player, constantly sharing your ideas with the other commanders around you, and help create a positive climate amongst your peers.

Get off your duff and make the time to meet with and/or to write letters to the one or two officers who most impressed you but are currently stationed elsewhere. Seeking out knowledge from those around you is one simple thing you can do that will have a tremendous impact on your time in command.[3]

Summary

You must be committed to continual learning because if you aren't moving forward, you are moving backwards. This is true not only as you prepare for and command your unit, but even after you pass the guidon to the next commander. Learning includes organizing and thinking about command ideas, reading and reflecting, and actively soliciting input from experienced leaders around you. You owe it to yourself and your soldiers to do so with gusto.

---

[3] Prior to taking the guidon, we created a resource book of things like command philosophies, OER Support Forms, and Company TACSOPs. Log onto www.CompanyCommand.com to get all kinds of great ideas from current and former company commanders. We also encourage you to contact recent company commanders directly via the "Cmd Contacts" section of the Web site. Don't miss an opportunity to be better prepared to command your unit!

Section 2. Natural Laws of Leadership

You may not believe in gravity or even be aware of it. However, when you drop a rock, it still falls.[4] Similarly, there are laws that govern our ability to lead effectively. They appear obvious and yet, because they are so often disregarded, we feel compelled to share them with you in this section. Moreover, these "laws" help clarify our approach to command in all areas from leader development to training to building a positive command climate. It doesn't take much to agree that they are true, but it takes a lot to have the discipline required to align yourself with them. It is the difference between success and failure.

The Farming Law

The farming law—**you reap what you sow**—is obvious but regularly ignored. A farmer who wants to reap a productive harvest in the fall must plant in the spring and work the fields through the summer. Just like it would be ridiculous for a farmer to skip all the hard work and still expect to harvest, there are no short-term fixes in creating winning teams.

- If you want to do well on the PT test, you must overload on pushups and sit-ups and focus your running on "speed work" far enough out to reasonably achieve the results you desire. The leader must plan the PT test at the most opportune time (you will never find the perfect time), communicate the fact that the PT test is coming up, issue the challenge to excel (most soldiers will rise to a challenge), and then ensure everyone remains focused on the goal until the test date arrives.

- If you want to be ready during the "Squad Enter and Clear a Room Live Fire" that is coming up, you have to conduct quality leader training to ensure that all your leaders are

---

[4] Stephen R. Covey. *Principle Centered Leadership*, 1990: p. 18.

on the same sheet of music and prepared to train their soldiers. What are the individual skills that must be understood in order to do well at the collective task? Do we have a company SOP on this training that is clearly understood by all the leaders? Remember that an SOP is not an SOP until it is known and understood by all. If you want to really frustrate your squad leaders, let them train their soldiers for half a day until you see that you don't like some of their techniques and then pull the leaders together to figure out the way you want to do business.

• If you want to excel on marksmanship, quit "checking the block"; develop a quality program that builds from the basics and gives the soldiers time on the trigger.

Quick fixes rarely fix anything! Leading, like farming, is hard work. The harvest—victory on the battlefield, changed lives, tomorrow's leaders—makes the hard work worthwhile.

The 24-Hour Law and the Big Rocks Metaphor

Ok, we know that there just isn't enough time to do it **all**. In fact, the 24-hour law—**there is a finite amount of time in a day**—tells us that it *all* can't get done. However, if you have figured out what the "big rocks" are for your outfit, you can be focused on what is important and not waste time worrying about what doesn't really matter in the long run. Stephen Covey, in his book *First Things First,* tells a story that explains what a big rock is.[5] At a seminar, the instructor pulled out a jar and asked the students how many rocks he could fit in the jar. After filling up the jar with rocks, he asked if it was full. Of course, it appeared to be full until he poured a large cup of gravel into the jar. After then pouring another cup of fine sand into the jar, the students began to understand the point he was making:

---

[5] Stephen R. Covey, A. Roger Merrill and Rebecca R. Merrill, *First Things First,* 1994: p. 88-89.

Figure out the important things and put them in your life first (*first things first*).

The alternative is to let the "small" but often urgent stuff fill up the jar, not allowing any of the big rocks to fit in at all. We have talked to several commanders who were frustrated following their time in command. They felt as if they were treading water during their commands and were never able to accomplish the things they intuitively knew were important. They had allowed the urgent but not really important things to dominate their calendars.

Put the "big rocks" in first   **Otherwise, your jar will fill up with sand**

Of course, first you must actually know what the big rocks are. Once you know what they are, place them on the calendar, to include everything that must come first to make it a quality product/event—something that will yield superior results. The things that are not big rocks for the outfit will often still need to get done; however, you will purposefully not invest the same time and effort into them. The key to success here is communication with the company and, if necessary, with your boss. If your leaders are a part of developing what the big rocks are in the company and fully understand what is going on, they will no longer be frustrated when a "little rock" event isn't so hot. In fact, they will be motivated because they will have a newfound sense of satisfaction knowing that the things they think are important are being planned and executed to a high standard.

This is not a new idea for the Army. The METL concept goes right along with this approach. Hone down the myriad of tasks that we train on to the few collective tasks that are the most important: the "big rocks" for the outfit.

It sounds pretty simple. However, it takes truly disciplined planning and hard work to ensure you allocate time on the calendar for those things that build towards a successful event, whatever that event may be. Remember that—like the farmer— you will reap what you sow.

You can always see people's real priorities by the way they spend their resources—if you look at their calendars and checkbooks, you can identify the real priorities. The same is true for your unit. Look at your calendar and other resources to see if there is alignment between your vision and where your resources are going. If there is not alignment, it is time to make some changes. Too often we jam stuff onto the calendar because it briefs well or sounds like a great idea, but it simply does not fit within the unit's vision. If it doesn't fit, get rid of it—period, with no looking back. **Just as you tailor a soldier's load for the mission, so you must tailor your calendar to fit your vision. Be careful not to put too much in your "rucksack."**

On this note, before you take command ask yourself this question: "What are those things that only I can and must do in my role as commander?" We think it is important that you wrestle with this question, and then get feedback from a friend or mentor who has commanded already. Every commander will have a different answer—the key is to identify these items and then turn your subordinate leaders loose on the other things. Ensure a "system" is established for each of the critical aspects of your unit and that someone is responsible to manage that system (i.e., "pin the rose" on someone). We referred to the areas that we were not going to delegate responsibility for as our "big three." Here is one example of a commander's "big three": Leader Development/Leader Training, Training Management, and Physical Fitness. There are only 24 hours in a day, 365 days in a year. Figure out what is really important and put your energy into getting it done.

Summary

In this section we have talked about natural laws and have used the farming law, the 24-hour law, and the "big rock" metaphor to bring out some fundamental truths that apply to effectively leading your organization. Commitment to excellence will require the discipline to prioritize, plan, and inspire your subordinates to do the same. This is what great company-level leaders do.

Section 3. Vision

"There is no more powerful engine driving an organization toward excellence and long-range success than an attractive, worthwhile, and achievable vision of the future, widely shared."[6]

Know Yourself First

The first Army Leadership Principle is *know yourself and seek self-improvement.* We believe that the know-yourself part of this principle is fundamental to your success as a leader and is the beginning of creating vision. If, in fact, self-knowledge really is the basis of all other knowledge,[7] leaders must take time out to study themselves. You do this by reflecting on where you have been and who you are, by considering what is really important, and by imagining the future. A perfect time to do this is during your Captains' Career Course, and it is especially important just prior to assuming command. If we were kings for a day, we would give every captain two weeks off prior to taking command. These weeks would be a time to reflect and prepare for the upcoming journey. Of course, this rarely happens;

---

[6] Burt Nanus, *Visionary Leadership*, 1992: p. 3.
[7] Stephen Covey, *Seven Habits of Highly Effective People*, 1989: p. 40.

instead, officers are usually rushed from one job to the next. All too often, captains continue to be weighed down with "urgent" issues in their current staff jobs even while they conduct inventories and prepare to lead their new companies. Force yourself to take at least a long weekend prior to taking command to read, reflect, imagine, and mentally prepare for the challenge ahead.

The Army's 11 Leadership Principles[8]

1. **Know Yourself** and Seek Self-Improvement
2. Be Technically and Tactically Proficient
3. Seek Responsibility and Take Responsibility For Your Actions
4. Make Sound and Timely Decisions
5. Set the Example
6. Know Your Soldiers and Look Out For Their Well-Being
7. Keep Your Soldiers Informed
8. Develop A Sense Of Responsibility In Your Subordinates
9. Ensure That The Task Is Understood, Supervised, and Accomplished
10. Train Your Soldiers As a Team
11. Employ Your Unit In Accordance With Its Capabilities

Self-Study Techniques

It is easy to say that you need to study yourself; it is much more difficult to actually do so. Here are a few techniques that may help you reflect, know yourself better, project forward, and envision the future. We recommend doing all of them and even sharing your personal insights with a friend. The first technique to get you started is to write down what you think makes a great commander. You could write a short essay or just brainstorm on paper using bullet comments. Think back to those leaders who had a positive impact on you and consider why they were effective. After the list is complete, take a break. When you

---

[8] "Leaders who view these principles as the bedrock of their leadership will build effective units—composed of soldiers with skill and will who work together as a team to accomplish the mission." Dandridge M. Malone, *Small Unit Leadership*, 1983: p. 34.

come back to it, eliminate all but the top five attributes. You are imagining the ideal commander. If you get stuck, think about those things that make a "bad" commander to get you going again. This process helps you to see what you value in a leader and helps you envision what you want to be like as a commander.

What makes a commander?	
Ideal Commander or Leader	**Bad Commander or Leader**

Another exercise is to write out your strengths and weaknesses. Remember that no one will see this, so be honest with yourself. What are you good at? What are you passionate about? What gets you really excited and gives you great satisfaction? "People's passions flow naturally into creating something that truly excites them."[9] What contribution would you be excited about making? We believe that you can make the greatest difference in your company by understanding your strengths, and then making full use of them whenever possible.

What are you not so good at? What gets you angry or sets you off? What one thing frustrates you the most? Understanding your weaknesses will help you to know what areas you need to improve upon, what areas you might delegate, and what types of subordinates would help round you out. If you are honest and identify areas that need improvement, you can decide to change and take steps towards growing as a leader.

---

[9] Peter Senge, "The Practice of Innovation," *Leader to Leader Journal*, Summer 1998: p. 5.

Knowing Myself	
Strengths	**Weaknesses**

Comparing and contrasting the results of these first two exercises might prove valuable to you as you seek to better know yourself.

Remember that those things that are strengths can in fact become weaknesses in different circumstances. A great leader will consider how a new job and a different situation might require a leadership approach different than what worked in the last job or circumstance.

One other powerful way to understand yourself as a leader is to imagine that you have completed your command. Your soldiers, NCOs, and officers are hanging out talking about you. What would you *like* them to say about you? Take the time to write out what you would ideally like each of them to say. Once you are finished, think through what you will actually need to do in order to get to that idealized end state. You might find it beneficial to expand this exercise to include your 1SG, fellow company commanders, your battalion commander, and any other important people in your life. This exercise has the potential to clearly show you what you think is important. In addition, the results can serve as an azimuth by which you evaluate your future actions.

What would I want them to say about me?	
Reviewer	**Comments**
Soldiers	
NCOs	
Officers	

Have a designated notebook for these ideas, so that they are organized and handy. During your time in command, you can review the notebook and add to it using real examples that will help you understand yourself in an even deeper way. This self-reflection throughout your time in command will serve as a sort of personal azimuth check.

Finally, we encourage you to share the results of your self-study with a trusted friend or mentor. This will be especially valuable if this person has already commanded a company.

Vision Framework

What kind of company do you want to be a part of creating? As you continue preparing for company command, you will want to start thinking seriously about this question. The depth of your self-knowledge will play a big part in your ability to effectively do this. We believe that you should develop your personal vision for command, and then, once you take command, take your leaders through this same process in order to create a compelling, shared vision. The vision framework that has worked for us and that we will take you through is:

Vision = Purpose + Envisioned Future + Core Values [10]

We began this section on vision with a great quotation that communicates the power that vision can have on a unit. But so what? How does this apply to you personally?

Exceptional leadership is always rooted in genuine, passionate commitment. Exceptional units emerge when the people of the unit are passionately committed to what they are doing. On the one hand, there is the leader—you—and on the other hand, there are the followers—your soldiers. Where does the passionate commitment that you find in exceptional leaders

---

[10] See Peter Senge, "The Practice of Innovation," *Leader to Leader Journal*, Summer 1998; and Collins, James and Jerry Porras, *Built To Last: Successful Habits of Visionary Companies*, 1994.

and units come from? It always begins with vision. The next two sections will provide you some practical ideas on how you can uncover vision in yourself—personal vision—and in your company—shared vision. We believe the process will unleash the kind of passionate commitment that you want in your company.

Personal Vision: Purpose, Envisioned Future, Core Values

First, ask yourself, "What is the **purpose** of the unit I am going to command?" Why does the unit exist? Vision that is not grounded in a clear purpose will often be arbitrary and lack meaning, so spend some quality time thinking through this important question.

What is the purpose of my unit?

Second, **envision the future**. Vision can be defined as "a picture of the future we seek to create."[11] One way to get at this is to describe a great unit. What is it like? An even more powerful way to get at this is to describe a unit that you would be excited about being in. Fill in the blank in this statement: If my company is like _____, I will really be inspired. Imagine the future and ask yourself why someone would want to be in your company. This activity will help you get at what you value, and it will begin to tap into your own passionate commitment.

---

[11] Peter Senge, "The Practice of Innovation," *Leader to Leader Journal,* Summer 1998: p. 5.

> # Envisioned Future: The unit I would be psyched about commanding.

Imagine that it is one year from the day you take command. You just ran PT with one of your squads, walked around your company area, watched a platoon live-fire exercise, and attended a company party. Pick up a pen and paper and describe what you witnessed. You are envisioning what you would like your unit to "look like, feel like, and be like when you and others have completed the journey."[12]

The third part of building your vision is defining **core values**. Core values describe how the company wants life to be on a day-to-day basis while pursuing the vision. Ask yourself, "How do we want to act, consistent with our purpose, along the path toward achieving our vision? Core values are only helpful if they can be translated into concrete behaviors."[13] What are the most important values of this company? Brainstorm and then hone down your list, seeking to make it as succinct as possible. You want to create a focused beam of light—a set of values that are truly "core" and clearly define how the company lives—that can burn a hole through a wall. Avoid a laundry list of values that diffuses the light and weakly illuminates an entire wall.

> # What are the core values that drive behavior in this company?

---

[12] James Kouzes and Barry Posner, *The Leadership Challenge*, 1995: p. 96.
[13] Peter Senge, *The Fifth Discipline*, 1990: p. 224.

Is this hard work? Yes—and well worth every minute of it! Some will read this and wonder if anyone actually does this kind of stuff. Is it too "touchy, feely"? We believe that awesome units begin with leaders who are passionately committed to an attractive and worthwhile vision. This is where exceptional leadership begins.

In fact, there are hundreds of examples of commanders who are doing or have done exactly what we have described here and, in the process, have inspired some heroic results. Two examples from our not-too-distant past include a company commander during the Korean War, Ralph Puckett, and a battalion commander during the Vietnam War, Hal Moore. We have had the privilege of listening to both speak; most of you will know the latter from his book, *We Were Soldiers Once...And Young.*

Colonel (Retired) Ralph Puckett, Ranger Hall of Fame inductee, gives an inspiring talk about his experience building a winning team of warriors during the Korean War.[14] While still a 1LT, he was selected to command the newly formed 8th Army Ranger Company. He built a combat-ready team from scratch, and he led it until he was seriously wounded. When he tells you about his personal vision for what he wanted the company to be, you feel his passionate commitment bursting out; we would have loved being in his unit! Quite simply, he told his company,

We are:
- **Physical Tigers**
- **Tactically and technically proficient**
- **A Killing Machine**
- ***The* best unit—every soldier believes it!**

He went on to say that company commanders build winning teams by setting and demanding adherence to high standards, concentrating on fundamentals, and creating a unit climate where every soldier is comfortable providing feedback focused on improving everything, including the CO's performance. Finally,

---

[14] Colonel (Retired) Ralph Puckett, speeches at Ft Benning, Georgia on 1 February 1995 and Schofield Barracks, Hawaii on 11 January 1996.

he recommended stressing the leaders during training so that they would be prepared for the high stress that comes during combat.

Hal Moore took over 1st Battalion, 7th Cavalry having already developed a vision for what a great battalion would look like. In *We Were Soldiers Once...And Young*, LTC Moore describes his first day in command: "In a brief talk to the troops afterward I told them that this was a good battalion but it would get better. 'I will do my best,' I said. 'I expect the same from each of you.'" His vision was to build a winning team. He began communicating this from the day he took command. In his first talk with the officers of the battalion, he gave this guidance:

> Only first-place trophies will be displayed, accepted, or presented in this battalion. Second place in our line of work is defeat of the unit on the battlefield, and death for the individual in combat.[15]

You can imagine the energy he created during his first day in command. Of course, he went on to live his creed and to inspire a shared commitment to victory. Read *We Were Soldiers Once...And Young* and you will see how LTC Moore's vision impacted the soldiers and leaders of the battalion and led to incredible results in combat.

Tony Nadal commanded Alpha Company during the battle of LZ X-Ray. In his comments below you will find further insight into how LTC Moore created a winning team, and just some plain old good advice for up-and-coming company commanders:

> He did have a clear vision of wanting to command the best battalion in the Army, and he quickly set the tone. He often reinforced his views in talks to his officers and troops. His comments about no second-place trophies permeated everything that the battalion did. He was always leading by example, setting the tone, and demanding the best. One of his most important messages

---

[15] Harold G. Moore and Joseph L. Galloway, *We Were Soldiers Once...And Young*, 1992: p. 18-19.

before we deployed to Vietnam was that no soldier, dead or wounded, would be left on the battlefield. This was very important to the soldiers and we indeed acted on that value. One of his characteristics was to always be where the action was the hottest and not to expect nor accept creature comforts that his soldiers didn't have. One of the messages all new commanders have to realize is that command is a position of responsibility, not privilege.[16]

You must capture this same passionate commitment as you describe what you want your company to be like. Do you want to command an awesome unit? Then begin imagining what that unit will be like. The stories of Puckett and Moore are part of our rich heritage; your story will become a part of our history too. What will your legacy be?

You will want to take the guidon having already done what we have described here—unleashing your own passionate commitment by developing a clear sense of purpose, picture of the future, and core values. In addition, you will want to take command ready to articulate this to your unit. Publishing a command philosophy and conducting initial meetings with your leaders and soldiers are methods to immediately begin communicating your vision and passionate commitment.

We are both infantry officers, and we planned on taking command of rifle companies. While at the Captains Career Course, we began developing our personal vision for command. We started by thinking through the purpose of our units. In a rifle company, it is easy to understand that the bottom line is killing the enemy, and it doesn't take much convincing to get your soldiers to see this. Soldiers want to be on the winning team, plain and simple. The driving question for us as we considered company command became: "What does a winning rifle company look like?"

Based on our experience, we knew that success in any organization hinges on *Leadership.* "The strength of any organization is a direct result of the strength of its leaders. Weak

---

[16] Tony Nadal, interview with Nate Allen and Tony Burgess, 24 February, 2001.

leaders equal weak organizations. Strong leaders equal strong organizations. Everything rises and falls on leadership."[17]

Once we clarified leadership as the force that would power our winning team, we worked to describe the other key components that make up a winning team. After many drafts and a lot of energy spent, we concluded that **winning teams are disciplined, fit, and motivated.** To win, we had to be *Disciplined* and able to perform our mission. The Latin root word of the word discipline means "to learn" and implies that disciplined units are learning units that pay the price required to develop skilled competence. A common theme running through all accounts of combat is the need to be *Physically Fit.* Combat veterans almost to the man comment on how much more incredibly exhausting combat is, both physically and mentally, than they could have imagined. If your soldiers are going to grab the enemy by the nose and kick him in the tail-end, they must be physical maniacs. Finally, great combat teams are *Motivated.* This is driven by loyalty, teamwork, and care for one another and the knowledge that each individual is a meaningful part of something significant.

Out of all this flowed a vision statement that inspired us as we continued to prepare for command: **We are a winning team: a cohesive band of disciplined, fit, and motivated warriors that can destroy any enemy.**

Pictures often say more than words alone. We used a wheel metaphor to help us communicate our vision (see diagram below). Because leadership would power our team and make all forward movement possible, the hub of the wheel represented it. The main spokes of the wheel represented the other components of our winning team framework. Using the metaphor, one can see how bumpy the ride might be if one of the spokes is out of alignment or not as strong as it needs to be. And you can see that no movement would be possible at all without leadership.

---

[17] John Maxwell, *Developing the Leaders Around You*, 1995: p. 6.

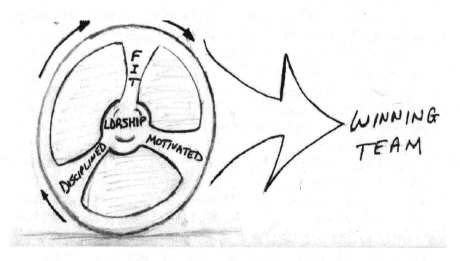

We arrived in command ready to articulate this for the company. Our passionate commitment couldn't help but shine through because we were so excited about what we were doing. The day we assumed command, we provided our leaders with a memorandum that described our vision (see an example on page 57). The memo served to focus our own thinking about command. In addition, it communicated where we wanted to take the company. We used this same framework—leadership driven, disciplined, fit, and motivated—in our initial meetings with the soldiers and leaders, in our initial counseling sessions, as the basis for our OER support forms, and in the way we framed our company goals.[18] This book, by the way, is organized in the same way.

Shared Vision: Purpose, Envisioned Future, Core Values

Ok, first you develop your personal vision and take the guidon ready to begin communicating that vision. Since your personal vision is really about who you are and what you think is important, everything you do will end up communicating it (hopefully, who you are and what you think is important are

---

[18] Another framework that many officers use for OER support forms is: Leading, Training, Maintaining, Caring. We are not necessarily advocating our framework, but we do believe it is critical to have one.

aligned). However, you will at the same time want to shift your efforts towards developing a *shared* vision. Are we contradicting ourselves here? No, our experience proves otherwise.

Leaders with a vision provide an azimuth and create energy about what the team stands for. However, their biggest challenge is communicating the vision in such a way that it inspires the organization. Imposing your vision might not be the best way to tap into your unit's passionate commitment. The latent energy of the outfit might best be unleashed when the vision—purpose, envisioned future, and core values—comes from within your soldiers themselves. Peter Senge underscores this approach: "The practice of a shared vision involves the skills of unearthing shared pictures of the future that foster genuine commitment and enrollment rather than compliance."[19]

What we are suggesting is that you take your leaders through the same process that you personally went through. Have them think through and articulate purpose, envisioned future, and core values. Not only will this tap into their passionate commitment—it will also further energize you and ensure your ideas are on track. If you are questioning this approach, just turn the tables and imagine how inspired you would be if your boss went through this process with you. At the end of the day, we are most committed to those things that we are part of creating. Let your soldiers be a part of this creation process, and you will be absolutely amazed at the results.

Your work should result in some kind of overall statement that describes the company vision. Write this in terms that soldiers can relate to—use words and images that are meaningful to them. Post the vision statement in front of the company and refer to it at every opportunity (key training events, when confronted with change, during AARs and training meetings, etc.) You can see how much more powerful it will be if the unit creates the statement rather than you telling them what it is. Here is an example of the vision statement and core values that Nate and his leaders developed:

---

[19] Peter Senge, *The Fifth Discipline*, 1990: p. 9.

Example Company Vision

QUICKSTRIKE VISION:

Quickstrike is a cohesive band of warriors who are disciplined, fit, and motivated. We possess the skill, will, and teamwork required to destroy any enemy.

CORE VALUES:

- We are known as Live Fire Experts
- Our PT program is Battle Focused. We create physical maniacs.
- We care for our soldiers and families with a passion.
- We are known for our disciplined field craft.
- Our officers and NCOs are renowned for their hard-nosed discipline and expertise.

Nate then had his platoon leaders take the refined company vision statement and core values and, with their respective platoon leadership, draft the same for their platoons, thus taking it down to the lowest level of the outfit and creating alignment within the organization.

Remember that the initial concept is a starting point and not the *end-all* answer. Too many command philosophies and vision statements are published on day one and are never referred to again. Leadership is a process, just as creating a vision is a process that will continue to develop during your command. Therefore, do not worry about creating the "perfect" statement. The ultimate sign of success here is that the vision becomes a part of your unit culture and helps you move towards the future you desire. Use the vision statement to guide your decisions, and it will become an energizing factor in your organization. Leaders who put a memo on the wall speak softly; leaders who actually make daily decisions based on the unit vision create a deafening roar.

In closing, it is important to note that an inspiring, shared vision will "pull" you into the future if and only if you have the discipline to continually compare it with your current reality. We recommend—at a minimum of once a quarter—evaluating whether your team is in alignment with the vision (See Leader Azimuth Check, page 71). Continually ask yourself if the unit goals and priorities, allocation of resources, and award and recognition program reflect who you say you are. Then have the courage to change what needs to be changed.

Summary

Knowing where your unit is going is critical to arriving successfully. The Roman philosopher Seneca put it like this: "You must know for which harbor you are headed if you are to catch the right wind to take you there." We believe the first step in figuring out "your harbor" is self-study that is focused on understanding what you think is most important. In many ways, your company will reflect who you are; your personal effectiveness will impact how effective your company can be. Take command ready to articulate your vision for the company, but understand that your real goal is to create a shared vision that taps into the passionate commitment of all your soldiers.

Section 4. Initial Unit Assessment

Before you can lead an organization, you need to understand it. Although it is critical that you take command having already developed a personal vision for command, the way that you articulate it and begin building a shared vision will be impacted by the dynamics that already exist in the unit. Perhaps you will find that the unit is already in alignment with your philosophy. On the other hand, once you scratch the surface of the unit, you might find that the values that truly drive behavior in your company actually go against your own values. We are not saying that you should accept this, only that you must be aware of it. A well-planned initial unit assessment will help you understand current reality and can serve as a catalyst towards developing a shared vision and tapping into your soldiers' passionate commitment.

Although you might be able to assess the unit prior to taking command, in this section we will focus on assessing the unit once you take command. The techniques we give you will help you tap into the heart of the unit and get at the basic underlying assumptions that drive the organization. Using these techniques will clarify what is frustrating your soldiers and hindering success. This process will also lay the foundation for a good command climate because you are listening and using a team effort to identify the things that are good and bad in the unit. Finally, you will force the leaders to pause and reflect on what they think is most important.

Many of us have seen or used different types of written unit assessments, with different levels of effectiveness. The Army requires, as part of the Equal Opportunity (EO) Program, a unit assessment within the first 90 days of a new commander taking charge and annually thereafter. This standard survey is a series of questions that talks to EO, command climate, and general soldier issues. Although commanders can use this survey to find out information about key command-climate issues (especially if there is a "red flag" issue lurking out there), the process of internal written assessment could be used much more effectively. We will show you how to use the written survey to help transform your unit.

Most commanders meet with their soldiers right after taking command to officially introduce themselves and to talk about their priorities. This event is a "must" that sets the stage for the rest of your time in command.[20] Consider what you will say and ensure it is aligned with and communicates your personal vision. To get the most out of the process, the next step is to listen to

---

[20] Work with the outgoing commander and get this on the training schedule. When *you* are the outgoing commander, make sure this event is on the actual training schedule for the incoming commander.

your soldiers and take note of their concerns. Doing so establishes two-way communication and will begin to lay the foundation for trust simply because you care enough to listen. Moreover, you learn a great deal about the state of affairs in the unit. This process loses effectiveness the longer you wait. Within weeks, the soldiers will perceive you as part of the "problem" or the "them," and simply will not open up and be as honest with you. Don't miss this once-in-a-command opportunity.

Right after taking command, we spoke with the lower enlisted soldiers (EMs) and gave them a feel for who we were. We then gave the soldiers a butcher block and pens, and told them they had twenty minutes to write up the issues that were most important to them. We wanted to hear constructive input in the form of sustain and improve from the junior enlisted perspective. We could feel the energy moving in the room once they realized we weren't joking. We headed into another room where we met with the officers and NCOs of the outfit to tell them about ourselves and to hand out written questionnaires. Thirty minutes later, we returned to the EMs to find them still hard at work. At this point we had them brief us on their product to make sure that their intent was clear. You must seek to understand what they are really trying to say, which may be different than what they write. If there is something that is clearly not constructive, tell them right up front—they will respect you for it. Collect the butcher block and tell them that you will meet again the next month to review the issues and assess progress. This process was great fun and went a long way toward establishing rapport with the young soldiers in our new units. A good follow-up or update brief thirty days later is critical to establishing trust and showing them that the initial input was not just a "check the block" for you.[21]

The questionnaire we gave all the NCOs and officers of the unit really helped us understand the unit and helped us shape what we wanted to focus on right away. We found our leaders to be open, honest, and eager to share their ideas. Keep the questions simple and make sure you explain why you are doing

---

[21] A great technique is to use the same butcher block during your update brief to the soldiers.

this. There are many possible questions that will cause your leaders to think about the purpose of the unit and what needs to be changed to make the company better. See the example survey below to spark your thinking—keeping it to five or fewer questions will be more productive than having an overwhelming laundry list.

Although the survey itself is important, the real key is what you do with the comments. Right away, we collated similar responses and established several themes that appeared to exist in the unit. Next, we shared the results with the 1SG and other leaders in the outfit, keeping in mind that the responses might be misleading or just symptoms of problems. What you are really after is discovering the real, underlying causes to the issues; knowing them will allow you to begin effecting significant change right away. What you don't want to do is to fix one problem and create another. Quite often today's solutions are tomorrow's problems.

LEADER SURVEY

Directions: Please answer the following questions. Attach separate sheets of paper if you need more room.

- What do you think the bottom-line purpose of this unit is? Why do we exist?

- What do you like about this unit?

- What one thing is keeping this company from being even better?

- What is your biggest source of frustration in the unit right now?

- If the company were like _____, you would be excited. Describe what you would like the company to be like in the future.

Here are some other possible questions:

- What five or six words would you use to describe the character, feel, or spirit of this company?
- What words would you use to describe the kind of team you *want* to be on?
- What one thing would help give you more job satisfaction?
- What would you like to see more of?

In addition to helping us know and assess where our units were at, the surveys helped us look toward the future. Having the written comments put us in a great position to launch discussions about what is and should be important to the unit and what the direction of the outfit should be. Our young leaders were now thinking about what they thought was important to the unit and were discussing how the unit was or was not fulfilling their expectations. This reflection and dialogue is critical as you begin to communicate a vision for the outfit.

Looking back at the questionnaires over a year later, we were amazed at how much came out in the process. Almost every underlying problem in the unit was right there in black and white. Some of the issues were easy to tackle, while others took a lot of teaching, coaching, mentoring, and even personnel changes. The process was an invaluable tool that helped establish a road map for the future.

We end this section by underscoring that it is absolutely critical that you fully include your 1SG and executive officer in this process—positive changes will never happen without unity at the top.

Section 5. Unit Goals

Once you have a developed a shared vision and clearly understand the current state of affairs in your company, the next step is to develop unit goals that provide the outfit with specific things to work for. It is this step that takes good intentions—purpose, envisioned future, and core values—and translates them into action. When goals are aligned with vision, big things happen.

We developed goals that fell under each element of our command framework: Leader-driven, Disciplined, Fit, and Motivated. The company goals became the basis for our OER support forms. We had our platoon leaders develop platoon goals and had them use their platoon goals as the basis for *their* OER support forms.

We love the term Big Hairy Audacious Goals (BHAG) that James Collins and Jerry Porras describe in their book *Built to Last.*[22] General Patton once said, "If you never accept any challenges, you will never experience the exhilaration of victory." Moreover, "challenge is the motivating environment for excellence."[23] The term BHAG is about seeking out challenges and allowing them to be catalysts for inspiring performances. Soldiers consistently accomplish great things when they are challenged to do so. BHAGs are intensely challenging and may even appear insurmountable to *outsiders*—but your soldiers see them as tough but achievable.

Start by seeking out small victories in order to build momentum and a culture of achievement in the outfit. Keep your

---

[22] Collins, James and Jerry Porras, *Built To Last: Successful Habits of Visionary Companies*, 1994: p. 91-114.
[23] Teresa Amabile, "How To Kill Creativity," Harvard Business Review, Sep-Oct 1998: p. 53.

eyes open for opportunities to create momentum and talk up the great things that are happening in the outfit. Once soldiers see what can be accomplished, they will gain great confidence in the organization and will begin to see future challenges in a new light. Once a BHAG has been met, create another one in order to keep the outfit from becoming complacent and satisfied. This kind of thinking creates soldiers who step up to the plate, seek out challenges, think innovatively, and never cower in the face of tough odds. In combat, units will be faced with Big Hairy Audacious Goals—victory will always go to the unit that has accomplished great things during training and is therefore confident when faced with adversity in combat.

One can also describe a BHAG as a "stretch goal"—a goal that requires the organization to change how it operates. If you want to create change, you must enable your subordinates to think *outside of the box;* if the goal can be accomplished by operating in the same old way, your subordinates will not need to create innovative, new, and better solutions. In other words, if you want fundamental change, establish a goal that can be accomplished only if the outfit changes the way it does business. Only a BHAG or stretch goal will create the dynamic, innovative energy that causes great things to happen.

> Being invited to do better than we've ever done before compels us to reach deep down inside and bring forth the adventurer within...if leaders wish to get the best from others, they must search for or create opportunities for people to outdo themselves.[24]

This approach is the difference between seeking to avoid failures on the APFT and seeking to have the best average in the division. Your achievers will not be overly challenged or motivated to simply qualify on their personal weapon, but they might get excited if they are challenged to develop a marksmanship program that will yield 50% experts.

---

[24] James Kouzes and Barry Posner, *The Leadership Challenge*, 1995, p. 42.

29

Goal setting should be your leadership team's responsibility (together); however, you initially will need to push your leaders out of their comfort zones. Although soldiers will rise to meet challenges, they will not typically create goals that stretch them beyond their current capabilities and require them to think differently. Once your leaders have been energized around a stretch goal once or twice, they will begin to seek out challenges for themselves. Regardless of who creates the goals, the goals must be clearly communicated to the organization and must remain stable and well defined. You must be able to know when you achieve the goal; otherwise, it is no longer a goal.[25]

One last thought on unit goals: this isn't just about setting objectives and achieving them—it is about creating a climate in your organization that compels soldiers to embrace challenges and to rise to meet them with every available resource.

Don't underestimate the impact that your words have on your soldiers. Examine your speech patterns as you talk with your soldiers. Are you "playing to win" or "playing not to lose"? The difference between these two approaches has tremendous long-term consequences. Don't dwell in your communication on what you *don't* want to happen. Instead, focus your communication on what incredible things you *do* want to happen. When you tell someone not to lock the keys in the car, they immediately have an image of the keys being locked in the car, which can lead them to doing exactly what you did not want them to do. We challenge you to focus your guidance on the great things you expect your soldiers to do rather than on what you do not want them to do.

We close this section with two examples to get you thinking:

- Your unit is going into an operation in built-up terrain (MOUT) where there will be many non-combatants. Instead of demanding that "no civilians be shot," clearly articulate the rules of engagement (ROE) with a focus on accomplishment of the mission. The "playing not to lose" mind-set handicaps soldiers while the other frees

---

[25] Teresa Amabile, "How To Kill Creativity," *Harvard Business Review,* Sep-Oct 1998.

them in trust to handle each unique situation in the most appropriate manner.

- Your unit is stepping off on a five-mile run. Do you stand in front of this incredible group of soldiers and yell out, "No fall-outs!" This statement will automatically conjure up images of "falling out" in the minds of many soldiers, and it certainly won't motivate your physically fit troopers. Imagine if you stepped up in front of the company and read them a Medal of Honor (CMH) citation and then said, "Our objective this morning is a five-mile run. I need every single one of you on the objective. Victory, follow me!"

Are you fired up? We are!

Section 6. Managing Change and Transition

Change will happen—so don't fight it. Embrace it, and use it as an opportunity to build your team! We know that every organization goes through four stages during any transition:

D. PERFORM - If the change is managed well, the unit comes out performing at a high level with a renewed sense of team and trust.

C. NORM – Hopefully, healthy norms are established for how the unit performs and conducts itself, manages conflict, plans, etc.

B. STORM – Both the unit and individuals will express frustration with change and uncertainty as to how this change will affect them. Jockeying for position occurs, performance and motivation may decrease, creativity increases, and polarization occurs.

A. FORM – This is the change that starts the process. Examples include a change in goals, organizational mission or structure, personnel, or in the way things are done.

Your unit will experience this cycle many times throughout your time in command. It will happen when you take command, as your subordinate leaders rotate, and when your unit gets deployed. Finally, change that happens at the battalion and brigade level will impact the company too.

We believe that the way you respond to change will set the tone for your entire company.

If you understand that the "storm" phase accompanied by stress and uncertainty usually precedes the "norm" and "perform" stage, you will be much more likely to communicate confidence and a positive outlook that your subordinates will respond to. Kouzes and Posner put it this way: "Stress always accompanies the pursuit of excellence."[26] Being aware of this can radically alter the way you and your subordinate leaders manage change.

Clearly, the biggest change and transition that you will initially face is when you take command of your unit. Not only is this a big change for the unit, but also for you personally. We have already discussed some leadership tasks that will help you through this transition process, to include: having a clear vision; establishing and staying focused on the unit's core values; and setting and achieving short-term goals. In the final chapter of this book we will discuss how communication, trust, and team building are also crucial to leading organizations through change. In this next section, we will focus on a technique for planning your transition into command.

90-Day Agenda

Your move into command is a major change for the unit. You must have a plan to manage it. One great technique is to come into command with a three-month plan that lays out all the "big rocks" that you want to get established up front.[27] The first three months will become the bedrock for your future success, but you must have a plan. Initially, just come up with a generic 90-day plan, with one focus area per week. These are the areas that you want to check, establish SOPs for, and teach, coach, and mentor your leaders about.

As you draw closer to your assumption of command (preferably eight weeks out), you can begin taking your generic plan and laying it on the actual calendar. Once you complete

---

[26] James Kouzes and Barry Posner, *The Leadership Challenge*, 1995: p. 50.
[27] Steve Delvaux played a big role in developing this "90-Day Agenda" concept. While we were at the Infantry Officer Advanced Course (Now Captains Career Course), he spent hours with us brainstorming about how to build a winning team.

your initial unit assessment, you can further tailor your 90-day plan based on the specific needs and issues that you identify. For example, if you discover that your subordinate leaders are extremely frustrated with PT, you might move this up in your plan and address it right away. If you have a Division Maintenance Assessment coming up, you might adjust your plan so that you focus on maintenance right away.

Below is an example three-month plan. Right away the commander wanted to conduct an in-depth unit assessment using surveys and sensing sessions. In addition, counseling was one of his "big rocks," so he targeted this during the first month. As a part of that focus on counseling he ensured that there was a quality counseling SOP, leaders understood it, and they were actually following it. The company would deploy to the JRTC three months after he took command; therefore, several of the items on the 90-day agenda related to this. One example of a JRTC-related item was "knowing the enemy at JRTC." The commander brought in "experts" to teach classes on the enemy and held informal discussions and wargaming sessions with his leadership.

Month 1	Month 2	Month 3
Unit Assessment	PT SOP	JRTC-focused PT
Counseling Program	Company Tactical SOP	Know the Enemy (JRTC)
Training Mgt	Maintenance SOP	Deployment (POM, N-hr, etc.)
METL	OPD/NCOPD & Ldr Dev.	FRG & BOSS Newsletter

The chain of command knew what items were being addressed each week because the commander published his agenda up front. The end result was that SOPs were reviewed or developed from scratch, the company was very focused, and the commander's "big rocks" were implemented. The typical alternative is to come into command with no real plan and simply try to execute the previous commander's training schedule while you react to the overwhelming "urgent" things that dominate your days.

A crucial moment as you come into command is the meeting with your 1SG and XO in which you talk about roles and responsibilities. Spend a lot of time with them to ensure that all three of you are heading in the same direction and that you aren't duplicating work. In general, you should be focused on commanding and training the company, while the 1SG runs it, and the XO resources and maintains it. You must break down what that structure looks like with them and ensure that there is someone designated to be responsible for each critical system.

Leaving Command Side-Bar

Remember that the legacy of a leader is not where he is heading, but rather what he has left behind! Part of what you leave behind is the ability for the unit to function in your absence. For this to happen, systems, discipline, and initiative must be instilled—which requires a paradigm shift from managing your unit to leading and developing it, no matter what the cost. An additional mark of effective leaders is their ability to provide their units with a smooth transition to the next commander. As you prepare to leave command, take the initiative to get the next commander involved early on at meetings and by jointly developing a 90-day agenda. If you conduct a leader off-site azimuth check (See Leader Azimuth Check, page 71), take the incoming commander and let her run the planning portion for the training that she will be conducting with your unit. The incoming commander can listen in on all of the assessments and then give the unit initial guidance on the upcoming training—instead of having to go through that transition after taking command. It is all about what is best for your unit! Have new commanders review the vision to see if they feel comfortable with it, and help them get on board with where the unit is headed and what you are about as a team. You want the new commander to be successful!

Section 7. Ongoing Unit Assessment

It is easy to see how valuable a well-planned and thorough initial assessment of your unit can be. However, continual feedback throughout your command is just as important. General Sullivan, former CSA, understood the value of feedback and wrote specifically about the importance of surveys: "Polling is one more technique to communicate bottom up and then bottom down when you provide feedback to the outfit on the poll."[28] Searching out feedback that is tied to your unit vision and goals will take you to the "next level." As we mentioned earlier, you must have a clear picture of current reality if you expect to be aware of the changes you need to make to take you where you want to go.

An effective technique is to develop a quarterly survey that asks soldiers how well the unit is doing in those areas that the leadership agreed was important. This review is different than arbitrary surveys or sensing sessions because it solicits feedback on specific items. Moreover, it helps create a culture of accountability whereby the important things are clearly important. Avoiding problems never leads to success; surveys help the leadership come face to face with the issues that prevent the unit from being as good as it can be. Real learning happens when a person sees the gap that exists between reality and what they think is happening. Begin with leaders committed to the unit vision and goals, and then use polling as one method to help them see the "gap."

Let us say that one of your unit's "big rocks" is having a high-quality counseling program. Think of the impact you would have on the unit if you simply asked E4s and below if they are being given good feedback every month on what is expected of them and how they are performing. We are not talking about pointing fingers, but rather about creating another system to hold you and your leaders accountable for your goals—**the focus is how we can better live out the values that we have established.** Soldiers tell it like it is. They will give you great

---

[28] Gordon R. Sullivan and Michael V. Harper, *Hope Is Not A Method*, 1996.

insight into things that you and even their immediate leaders might never have known. They will also feel good knowing that you care about what they think and that their leaders will be held accountable and will be required to perform. Emphasize with the leaders that these are the soldiers' perceptions and not necessarily facts. This approach will help tone down leader defensiveness, and will help leaders accept the process. Polling does not take the place of leaders being where the rubber meets the road and observing what is happening; it is simply one more system that helps your unit achieve its goals.

For this technique to be effective, there must be a high level of trust between you and your subordinate leaders. MG William Boice once said, "When you are unsure of yourself, everything is threatening. When you are sure of yourself and know what you are doing, nothing is threatening." If you feel a lot of negative reaction from leaders on an issue, their frustration may be a sign that they are being developed. The goals of the unit are not optional, and the leaders are feeling the effects of being held accountable—either inspiration or frustration depending on their individual attitude and maturity. The next challenge for the leaders is to go through the same process with their subordinates. This is leader development!

Section 8. Leader Development

Your unit will rise only to the level of your leaders!

Dana Meade, a retired colonel and Vietnam veteran who has gone on to excel in the business world, wrote: "Leadership may be difficult to define, but we know that we cannot succeed without it, and that we will certainly recognize it by the exceptional results it produces."[29] Your number one priority as company commander must be developing the leaders who will produce exceptional results. Remember the wheel metaphor? Leadership is the hub that powers everything and allows forward movement in all other areas.

---

[29] Dana Meade in *Leading at Mach 2* by Steve Sullivan, 1995: p. 195

Before we move on and talk about some leader development *how-to's,* we must underscore the importance of your own character and of the way you treat your soldiers. You will never be able to inspire a shared vision or a commitment to leader development unless your subordinates trust you. Likewise, your subordinate leaders will find it difficult to develop *their* subordinates if they themselves are not trustworthy. This rule has been called the "First Law of Leadership: If we don't believe the messenger, we won't believe the message."[30] You can validate this "law" for yourself by thinking about your own experience— how you perceived the character of your leaders determined how willing you were to learn from them. Moreover, your subordinates will rise to your expectations of them. "Treat a man as he is and he will remain what he is. Treat a man as he can and should be, and he will become as he can and should be."[31] Your character and how you treat your soldiers will, in large part, define your ability to develop them.

A Concept for Leader Development

We have written this section as if you, the reader, are a company commander. Read it from that perspective, but also understand that this stuff applies to all levels of leadership. Here you will find a practical concept for leader development that can be applied immediately and will result in your leaders being better off for your having been a part of their lives.

Leader development may be considered the expansion of soldiers' individual capacities to lead.[32] Research has shown that leadership capacities are best developed through trial and error (actual experience)—but the research also points to several

---

[30] James Kouzes and Barry Posner, *The Leadership Challenge*, 1995: p. 26.

[31] Goethe, as quoted by Stephen Covey, *The Seven Habits of Highly Effective People*, 1989: p. 62.

[32] The Center for Creative Leadership (CCL) defines leadership development as "the expansion of a person's capacity to be effective in leadership roles and processes...leadership development is the development of capacities within the individual." McCauley, Cynthia D., Russ S. Moxley, and Ellen Van Velsor, ed. *The Center for Creative Leadership Handbook of Leadership Development*, 1998: p. 4.

mechanisms and catalysts that, when present, create the conditions for the most development to happen.[33]

Leader Development is Driven by <u>Experience</u>

We agree with this research and believe that the best way to develop as a leader is to actually lead. Leaders learn by leading, and they learn most when they are placed in a variety of challenging leadership experiences.

Military Experience Side-Bar

If you agree that developmental experiences are central to developing leaders, then you can see what an incredible opportunity it is to be a young person in the military. It is hard to think of another type of organization where a 22-year old person would get to lead in decentralized, challenging, multi-cultural, and sometimes extremely difficult circumstances. We are thinking of our own experiences like being a platoon leader and company commander during JRTC rotations, deployments to Saudi Arabia and Somalia, and the everyday personnel challenges that every officer faces. The fact that officers change jobs after one to two years reinforces the process of continued development. Add in schools like the Captains' Career Course and Command and General Staff College, and you have a progressive, experience-based model that other organizations can only dream of. Why do you think the business world so ardently seeks out young leaders with military experience?

Clearly the Army provides you some great leader-developing opportunities. However, we want you to see that your leaders

---

[33] See James Kouzes and Barry Posner, *The Leadership Challenge*, 1995; Morgan McCall, *High Flyers*, 1998; and McCauley, Cynthia D., Russ S. Moxley, and Ellen Van Velsor, ed. *The Center for Creative Leadership Handbook of Leadership Development*, 1998.

could develop their capacity to be effective leaders much, much more if you have a framework for understanding development and then implement specific plans to help them leverage learning from their experiences.

The simplest way we can think of to conceptualize how to leverage learning from experience is in the framework of **preparing for** the experience and **making sense of** the experience (See leader-development model below). As you learn how to better prepare your leaders for experiences and then help them process and make sense of their experiences, you will see significant development in your leaders. Moreover, as your subordinates develop, you will witness the exceptional results that effective leaders produce (i.e., your company will excel).

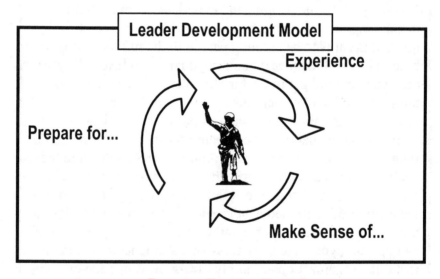

Prepare For the Experience

Preparing for the experience is critical. Think about the paradox that the more you know, the more you can learn. If leaders have thought through the upcoming experience, understand how it ties into the purpose of the unit and their own personal development, and know the doctrine that drives it, they will be in a position to learn a great deal. Contrast that scenario with leaders who go into the experience unprepared and try to learn simply by doing. Not only will these unprepared leaders learn less, but *their units* will also suffer because of it.

Tied into this is the individual leader's ability and motivation to learn. Simply said, a person must be open and motivated to learn from an experience, or else little development will occur.

Make Sense Of the Experience

The second element that leverages learning from experience is how we make sense of and process experiences. "Unexamined experiences don't produce the rich insights that come with reflection and analysis."[34] The Army AAR process is a great example of taking time to make sense of experience. Honest feedback and rigorous assessment are catalysts that bring out development.

"Leadership is, after all, a set of skills. And any skill can be strengthened, honed, and enhanced if we have the proper motivation and desire, along with practice and feedback, role models and coaching."[35] As a company commander, you will seek to strengthen, hone, and enhance the skills of your subordinates. Following their experiences, you can help them identify the "gaps" that exist in their set of skills and capabilities.[36] Seek to identify the gaps and then focus on how those gaps can be narrowed. This type of assessment is focused on development and is the beginning of preparing for the next experience. (See how this is a reinforcing process?)

It is important to note that there is often a delay between the experience and the "development." You shouldn't always expect instant growth in your subordinates; if you do, you will probably be frustrated. Like anything worthwhile, individual development

---

[34] James Kouzes and Barry Posner, *The Leadership Challenge,* 1995: p. 329.

[35] Ibid. p. 322.

[36] You can look for gaps in terms of the Army "Be, Know, Do" framework: **Be**: Who you are (character, values, attributes); **Know**: What you know (skills, knowledge, competencies); **Do**: What you actually do (actions and behaviors). These correspond directly to the Junior Officer Developmental Support Form (JODSF), which makes that an ideal form to use when developing a plan to close the "gaps."

takes time and a lot of work. Remember that, like the farmer, the leader-developer plants in the spring but may not harvest until the fall. As an example, your efforts with your lieutenants may not be fully "harvested" until they themselves are taking command.

The diagram below summarizes what we have talked about. We use the thick arrows to show how much more powerful the leader-development process will be when it is planned and occurs in the right environment.

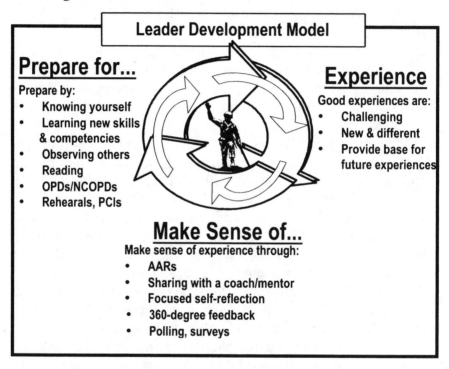

Leader Development Model

Prepare for...
Prepare by:
- **Knowing yourself**
- **Learning new skills & competencies**
- **Observing others**
- **Reading**
- **OPDs/NCOPDs**
- **Rehearsals, PCIs**

Experience
Good experiences are:
- **Challenging**
- **New & different**
- **Provide base for future experiences**

Make Sense of...
Make sense of experience through:
- **AARs**
- **Sharing with a coach/mentor**
- **Focused self-reflection**
- **360-degree feedback**
- **Polling, surveys**

The wonderful thing about leader development is that it is a continuous, reinforcing process that happens over time. The more your leaders develop, the better able they are to prepare for and make sense of their experiences, thus leveraging the most development from them. As the leader develops, he or she is better able to prepare for the next experience, and has a richer context with which to process new experiences.

Making Sense Side-Bar

There are some experiences that your subordinates are bound to misinterpret unless you step in and help them make sense of them—do not assume that you and your subordinates are processing an experience in the same way. When something bad or confusing happens (e.g., a training accident occurs, your unit does not accomplish the mission, or things just don't go the way you planned them), it is critical that you take the requisite time to talk with your leaders. We are excellent at AAR-ing collective training events, but we rarely take time out to "make sense of" and process other events that might be misinterpreted by young leaders. Don't leave this to chance—talk, communicate, coach, and mentor!

The leader-development process works best if it occurs within a learning environment. Imagine a unit where innovation and risk-taking are the norm, failure is not feared, and the focus is on growing and getting better instead of evaluating and weeding out. Challenging experiences will inevitably lead to some mistakes or failure. **How you deal with mistakes will define the learning environment in your unit**. The leader who sees failure as an opportunity to help junior leaders grow and develop will foster an environment that encourages stepping out of the "box" and trying innovative and new solutions. If you recognize that true *life-change* comes from times of either great joy or great pain, you can begin to see failure as an opportunity to develop leaders.

Think about your own training experiences to see this process in action. For example, let's say you were a battalion support platoon leader during a Joint Readiness Training Center (JRTC) rotation. This was an extremely challenging experience and probably would have developed you no matter what. However, in retrospect, you can see how your preparation and ability to learn, combined with feedback and assessment, significantly impacted your development. A positive and honest AAR process, self-reflection, and a battalion focused on growing rather than just evaluating helped you get the most out of the experience.

In summary, you can help develop your subordinates by making sure they get challenging, developmental experiences. Then, do everything you can to leverage learning by helping them prepare for and make sense of and process those experiences by providing and encouraging rigorous assessment and feedback.

Leader development will never *just happen*. Remember the "big rocks?" If it is important, then it needs to be scheduled on the calendar and deliberately planned. It is not enough to simply talk about it. And the company commander, more than anyone else, can impact whether or not there are specific plans for leader development in the unit for all leaders from the top to the bottom of her organization. We will now describe some practical ways that you can put talk into action.

Leader Development Put Into Action

Actions speak louder than words, so quickly move from talking about the importance of leader development to actually doing it.

Almost everything you do develops your leaders. From daily decisions you make, to on-the-spot corrections, to planning and executing training, to UCMJ actions—you are modeling leadership, and your leaders *will be* developed. However, in order to have the most powerful impact, you need to go beyond setting the example and role-modeling—you need to go into command having a clear leader-development philosophy, to include a specific plan of action. In this section, you will find some ideas to spark your thinking and inspire you to put theory into practice.

If, in fact, leader development is synonymous with personal development, one of the most significant things you can do is to require your junior leaders to study themselves (See Know Yourself First, page 9). Have them reflect on their own values and what is important to them. Studies show that having clarity about one's personal values leads to commitment much more so than does having clarity about the organization's values. When you help your subordinate leaders understand themselves—who they are and their own strengths and weaknesses—you unleash great energy in them. Moreover, self-awareness is a catalyst to self-improvement, which is what leader development is all about. When you and your subordinates become aware of the areas they need to improve—their "gaps"—you can develop a plan and create experiences to help them improve and close those "gaps." Likewise, as you become aware of their strengths, you can understand how to maximize their contributions to the team.

The absolute best way that you can develop your leaders on a regular basis is simply to use the chain of command when a problem arises. It sounds simple, but this principle is violated regularly—and no one thing will erode trust and leader accountability faster. Whenever there is an issue that involves a soldier, let the chain of command work. If you or your 1SG must address the soldier immediately, ensure that the squad leader is present or at least knows what is going on. Officers' tendency to be problem-solvers, combined with lack of time, makes it hard for them to step back and mentor others toward solving their soldiers' problems. If you and your 1SG make the commitment not to circumvent the chain of command, you will not only develop your leaders, but you will also keep responsibility where it belongs and prevent much unneeded frustration on the part of your leaders.

Another commonsense but often-missed way to develop your leaders is to block in time on the training schedule for leaders to do recurring but critical things to standard. Allocating and protecting adequate time for things like monthly counseling, pre-combat inspections, pre-marksmanship instruction (PMI), preventive maintenance checks (PMCS), and inventories will give your leaders critical experiences that are often done haphazardly due to high OPTEMPO and competing "urgent" demands. You can imagine the detrimental long-term effects when you consistently short-change your leaders in these areas.

A new lieutenant certification program is one method that will make a tremendous difference in the development of your platoon leaders. Not only will it focus new lieutenants; it will also serve to hold you accountable in developing them. This goes back to the importance of having a clear plan for leader development before you take command. Here is an example that you can modify and use for your own unit.

Example New Lieutenant Certification Program	
Task/Event	**Date Completed**
Set up and mark all equipment (TA-50 etc.) by SOP	
Qualify with M4	
Meet individual deployment requirements (SRF, POM etc.)	
Complete diagnostic APFT	
Complete LFX certification workbook	
Attend Range Safety Officer (RSO) and Range OIC class	
Complete OER Support Form/JODSF (67-9-1a)	
Brief Cdr on PLT Training and Personnel Status	
Conduct PSG/SL initial counseling	
Pass Company TACSOP written examination	
Pass call-for-fire test by FSNCO	
Pass radio exam to include constructing field expedient antennas	
Assemble/disassemble all platoon weapons w/function check	
Conduct PMCS on all platoon equipment	
Read the book *Small Unit Leadership*, and write paper	
Pass unit regimental history test	
Receive briefing from S4 on all supply procedures	
Brief XO on status of your additional duties	
Review PLT reception/integration SOP	

Moreover, make monthly officer and NCO professional development (OPD/NCOPD) a priority. This priority is the cornerstone of leader education in a company. Each monthly professional development session should be planned as well as any training event is, tied into the unit's purpose and goals, and part of an overall program. Ill-planned OPD/NCOPDs that don't fit into where you are going as a unit are really just a waste of time.

Tie to OPDs a professional reading program that requires reading and sharing of knowledge. One technique is to write a short summary of lessons learned and tips from the books you read, and then make copies to share with your squad leaders and above. Assign different books or articles to different leaders. .You can have an amazing impact on your young leaders simply by sharing the notes and ideas you get from reading relevant books and articles. If you don't take notes, you can still pass the book around or make copies of pages/chapters that you want your leaders to read. Subscribe to leadership journals and make sure that Army branch-specific magazines are being read every month.[37] If you find a book that inspires you and talks about what you think is important, having your leaders read it will help immensely in getting your team thinking on the same sheet of music. There is a synergistic effect that happens when your subordinates read a book that reinforces a concept you are trying to teach them.[38] Follow that up with experiences that reinforce this new thinking, and your leaders will develop dramatically.

Another excellent way to develop your leaders, and your unit overall, is to require your leaders to get out to observe training in other units. Have your platoon leaders attend a different company's training meeting. Send one squad leader from each platoon out to watch innovative marksmanship training being conducted by another unit in the division. When your leaders see outside of their little world, they will be able to look anew at your company. This experience will generate new and better ways of

---

[37] The Internet is a great way to get quality articles at no cost. *Leader to Leader* is an outstanding Leadership Journal that makes many articles available on their homepage. Have an LT run off one article a month for all your leaders to read. Not only will they learn a lot, but you will create important dialogue amongst your leaders. Check the "Cmd Reading" section of CompanyCommand.com for a list of journals and books that are available online.

[38] One of Tony's bosses in the 82nd, Tom Hiebert, had him read three books: Covey's *Principle Centered Leadership*, Moore's *We Were Soldiers Once...And Young*, and Rommell's *Attacks*. The impact was phenomenal.

doing business and will give your leaders great perspective on what your own unit is doing.[39]

Furthermore, requiring your leaders to plan future training is one of the best ways to develop them. If you are writing all of your unit's training plans, you are depriving your lieutenants of an opportunity to learn. If you are looking out far enough (See Leader Azimuth Check, page 71), you can assign all upcoming training events to a project officer and task him to provide the team a draft MOI for that event at the T-8 training meeting. You review it and give guidance by the T-7 training meeting so that it can be finalized and ready for resourcing by T-6.

Are you spending a lot of time doing things that aren't a part of your "big three"? If you are able to delegate the task, then delegate it. Yes, this often takes time because you have to train the individual on how to do it, but now you are developing your leaders! On top of that, you will now have time available to talk with soldiers, visit training, and plan future training. There are certain things that only a commander can do—no one else in the unit can perform these tasks. Focus on those things that only you can do and allow your leaders to do the other tasks.

Finally, any method you use to enhance feedback in your outfit will vastly improve leader development. Quality counseling will be the biggest catalyst. One-on-one counseling done on a regular basis that focuses on helping the leader make sense of past experiences and prepare for upcoming experiences will be the greatest ongoing activity that supports leader development. Use counseling as an opportunity to encourage and support innovation and risk taking and to challenge your leaders to seek out developmental experiences.

To get the most out of your developmental counseling, we recommend you spend some time prior to your counseling sessions thinking about leader development through the framework that we have described in this section of the book. We have applied that framework to the checklist you see below, in an effort to make it more practical. We believe that the impact

---

[39] Many will argue that there isn't enough time to do this. Change the way you look at things and you will be surprised how much time is out there. Support cycle is one great opportunity to *free up* some leaders to do this.

you have on your subordinates will be directly related to how much time you spend coaching and mentoring them through this process.

First, you will want to assess the learning environment in your unit:

The Learning Environment:
- Is risk taking and innovation encouraged?
- Are leaders afraid to fail, or do they view failure as a potential opportunity to grow and develop?
- Is assessment and feedback focused on growth and development or on evaluating and identifying winners and weeding out losers?

Next, use this checklist as a developmental guide for each of your subordinate leaders:

Lieutenant Checklist:
- Is he motivated to learn and grow?
- **Experience**:
  - What developmental experience has he had already?
  - What is the next critical upcoming experience?
  - What experiences would best develop him?
- **Prepare for the experience**
  - What is he good at? (Strengths and Natural Aptitudes)
  - What does he need to work on? ("Gaps"/Weaknesses)
  - How can he narrow the gaps that we know exist?
  - What is he reading right now that could impact preparation for upcoming experiences and narrow the gaps?
  - What formal training/education would help him prepare for the next key experience?

- **Make sense of and process the experience**
  - What did he learn from the experience?
  - What did not make sense, was confusing, or did not fit previous assumptions?
  - What are the "gaps" in effectiveness? ... as identified through:
    - Self Assessment
    - Others' Assessment and Feedback
      - 360-Degree Feedback
      - Surveys/Polling
      - Sensing Sessions
      - Feedback from you (the company commander)

After working through this checklist, you and your subordinate can then jointly develop a personal leader-development action plan. Effective leader-development action plans are intentional (planned and focused, not haphazard), purposeful (tied into the organizational vision), and personal. Fortunately, the Army has a fantastic "action plan" form ready for you to use; it is called the Junior Officer Developmental Support Form (JODSF).[40] For example, if one of your lieutenants has a "gap" in the area of public speaking—his lack of confidence in front of a group is preventing him from effectively communicating—then you might ask him what *specifically* he plans to do to close the "gap." Some effective action plan bullets on the JODSF might look like this:

- Read two books on public speaking NLT 1 October.
- Give the company safety briefing on Friday, 5 October.
- Videotape next platoon operations order briefing (9-10 October platoon LFX)

---

[40] *FM 22-100 Army Leadership* and the developmental counseling web page (http://www.counseling.army.mil/) are both awesome resources for counseling that lay out how to counsel effectively and use both the JODSF and the Army developmental counseling form (DA Form 4856-E). Of note, the counseling form has a section called "Plan of Action" and a section for leaders to clarify their responsibilities in implementing the plan of action.

Encourage your lieutenants to develop their own action plans, but provide coaching and mentoring through the process. Then regularly review this process, have the lieutenants update the JODSF at least quarterly, and hold them accountable to their plans. Finally, when you counsel your subordinates, ask them to talk you through *their* subordinates' leader-development action plans.[41] You are modeling the type of counseling you want them to do. In addition, you are requiring them to tell you, in specific terms, how they are developing their own subordinates.

Executive Officer Development

You have a special responsibility to develop your executive officer (XO). Make it a goal to prepare your XO for command by providing her with experiences and then helping her make sense of the experiences. You are the mentor that can have the biggest impact. Her future time in command will be influenced by everything she sees you do. The other reason that developing your XO is critical is that in combat she will inevitably have to take over, whether you are injured, at a Battalion OPORD, or simply conducting decentralized operations. Her effectiveness will be directly related to the experiences that you have given her during training.

During the course of your command, there will be times when your XO will have to take over simply because you are not available. However, you will also want to ensure that she gets opportunities to take over when you *are* around. Let the XO run a training meeting and then work with her afterwards on what could have been done better. The most dramatic impact you can have on her future will be in tactical operations. Allow her to plan and execute several missions during your time in command.[42] The XO is extremely busy, so if you don't force her

---

[41] For NCOs, the NCOER form and the developmental counseling form are great tools to accomplish this.

[42] Tony can remember in detail every company operation that Martin Reutebuch, his company commander, let him lead while he was the XO. Not only was Martin mentoring Tony, but he also was inspiring a lasting trust and commitment.

to do this she may come up with a list of the "urgent" things that prevent her from doing it. One technique is to follow behind her on an operation and handle all calls to battalion while she runs the company. Or, you might tell the battalion commander what you are doing and let your XO do all the talking. Do what works, given the dynamics in your battalion.

One of your greatest legacies will be how effective your subordinates are as they command their own companies. For your XO, this opportunity could happen within a year or two upon leaving your unit; in combat, it could be much quicker. As you draw up a specific list of goals for your time in command, include the development of your executive officer with specific bullets like, "She will plan and execute at least two company tactical operations."

Leader Training (Enabling Training)

Leader development is the ongoing process of growth leaders undergo throughout their careers, with an emphasis on process and potential. Leader training, a critical sub-element of leader development, is focused on preparing leaders to conduct specific upcoming collective training events.

If training is the Army's priority, then leader training has got to be one of your top priorities. Planned, hands-on leader training prior to collective training will make the difference between great and mediocre training. The long-term impact will mean the difference between being a winning team or a losing team.

A great way to conduct leader training is to start with an open-book written test given a week before any collective training event. This test can be developed by one of the platoon leaders or platoon sergeants and should cover all of the doctrine, company SOPs, and TTPs related to the training event. Take a hard look at the collective tasks being trained and then test those and the supporting sub-unit collective, leader, and individual tasks. One technique would be to post the top three scores for everyone to see (consider giving a three-day pass to the squad whose leaders' combined scores are the highest in the company).

Ensure the low-scoring leaders are re-tested, counseled, and developed so that they raise their knowledge level prior to the training event.

Then, the Friday before the training event, release your soldiers early and have the team leaders and above conduct hands-on training focused on the tasks to be trained the following week. This can be done using Omega-type training where leaders operate one level down as a unit performing the tasks. Or, based upon your situation, conduct instruction with each platoon giving classes on certain aspects of the training to be conducted using a round-robin approach. During this time, ensure you also train and re-validate your company SOPs that apply to the upcoming event. Implied here is that you iron out the company SOPs prior to the leader training.

For example, before our units conducted close-quarters battle training at the MOUT site, we gave a written test focused on doctrine, room clearing techniques, reflexive firing, and company SOPs. We then ran tape drills (white engineer tape replicating room layouts) with team leaders and above the Friday before training and showed video from the last MOUT LFX. Finally, the following week we started the training at team and squad level.[43]

Because of the vast difference in experience and knowledge that your leaders will have, it is crucial that you validate them through this process before every training event. We call this process learning the science. The first and crucial step must be that junior leaders understand the doctrine (grounded in the doctrinal basics and their weapons systems) and company SOPs—the science—and are thoroughly prepared for training. The practice of the art comes later as leaders know the science and apply it to their experiences. Too many leaders want to practice the art before understanding the science and they end up winging it, *hoping* things will turn out. The art will grow out of the science as they apply it.

---

[43] Imagine: The EMs have Friday off (they are motivated), the leaders are actually prepared for training (they are empowered), and everyone is excited during the actual training because it is quality training.

Quality leader training takes time and is hard work. Your leaders must be willing to sacrifice and pay the price up front in order to attain excellence. We call this a spirit of sacrifice— without it, you will quickly slip back into mediocre training. This spirit must start with you. Allocate time on the training calendar and hold your leaders accountable to properly preparing for training. A commitment to quality leader training will result in collective training that is *Super Bowl,* instead of *High School,* quality. Such a commitment will affect every aspect of your organization.

Chapter Summary

This entire first chapter on leadership is interwoven with leader development. Simply stated, you will never have exceptional leadership without a focus on leader development. Character and values and a commitment to those things that really matter are what drive success here. All of these things take time. However, it is time well spent and time that will make success in all the other areas talked about in this book possible.

As we close out this section, we want to end with a review of several key points that are the foundation for leader development. First, have a specific plan. Leader development is personal development. Personal development doesn't just happen; you need a specific development plan for the unit in general and for each of your subordinate leaders in particular. Remember the Farming Law—*You Reap What You Sow.* The seeds you sow as a leader in your soldiers' lives, whether for gain or loss, will produce fruit that the Army will reap for years to come. It is a process that takes great patience and wisdom. Too many leaders want to plant and harvest all in the same season.

Second, *more is caught than taught.* Your soldiers will care far more about what you say with your actions than with your words, so be very sure your actions match your words. It is hard for soldiers to believe the message if they do not believe the messenger. When you think you have the least influence might be when you have the most. The moment you think no one is watching and you take an action (right or wrong) is usually the moment when you are actually having the biggest impact. A soldier will observe you, and the effects will resound throughout your organization as no speech could ever do. What you *do* speaks so loudly that your soldiers won't hear what you *say*!

Leader development is driven by experience. In fact, challenging experiences and the ability to learn from them are the centerpieces of development. Preparing for experiences and making sense of them are the two critical ways we leverage the most learning. When this happens in the right environment, incredible leader development will occur.

In conclusion, leaders are responsible for developing their subordinates. However, leaders are also responsible for their own development. **Remember to continue to prepare for and make sense of your own experiences as you prepare for and command your outfit.**

Your Exceptionally Led Company

- Everything in your company hinges on your leadership.
- Spend focused time learning from experienced company commanders.
- Develop your personal vision for command—purpose, envisioned future, core values—and then take your leaders through this same process in order to create a compelling, shared vision.
- Develop big hairy audacious goals (BHAGs) that will ignite the fire of passionate purpose in your company.
- Prior to taking the guidon, develop a 90-day agenda.
- Conduct an initial assessment of your unit with a written survey.
- Figure out what the "big rocks" are and then put them on the calendar. Be aware of but don't worry about the "sand." You reap what you sow!
- Develop a leader development plan of action for the company as a whole and for each of your individual subordinate leaders.
- Experience is the central aspect of development; leverage learning for your leaders by helping them prepare for and make sense of their experiences.
- Conduct quality leader training down to team leader level prior to every collective training event.

Example Memorandum for Company Leaders
(Used in a light infantry rifle company)

SUBJECT: A Winning Team of Disciplined, Fit, and Motivated Warriors

1. Soldiers want to be on the winning team. After all, losing in combat leads to death. Our mission as the leaders of this company is to build a winning team. Leadership is the force behind all the things that make winning possible. If you imagine a winning team as a wheel, leadership based on values and principles is the hub that powers the wheel, while the spokes are discipline, fitness, and motivation. In this memorandum, I will give you some thoughts on leadership (the hub that drives the wheel), and my expectations for you to be disciplined, fit, and motivated.

2. First, be a **LEADER** of character. A leader knows where he wants the organization to go and he successfully communicates this vision to the organization. I want you to be an integral part of developing and communicating our vision.

   a. You will never be able to inspire a shared vision or communicate the core purpose/mission unless your subordinates believe in you. This has been referred to as the "First Law of Leadership: If we don't believe in the messenger, we won't believe the message" (Kouzes & Posner, 1995: 26). I believe that long-term success for Army leaders depends on who you are, and character is what drives this. Part of character is doing what you say and being congruent in word and deed (Integrity). Words whisper and example thunders, or as an old CSM once said, "The longer I live, the less I pay attention to what people say and the more I pay attention to what people do."

   b. Trust is the essential ingredient in any relationship, especially among soldiers. As I mentioned, doing what you say is critical. So also "trust is not about words; its genesis is the result of deeds" (Sullivan, 1996: 142). Trustworthiness is the foundation of trust; if you want to be trusted, you must be trustworthy. I look at trust as a bucket that is filled one eyedropper at a time. Another way to imagine trust is

57

a bank account that is best built by regular deposits (Covey, 1994). Ask yourself whether or not your behavior is making a deposit or a withdrawal in your subordinates' trust bank account. You can see that "who you are" will drive whether or not people will trust you over time. If your character is weak, no one will trust you; if no one trusts you, you are not a leader.

    c. Leadership is the hub that powers the wheel or the force that drives the success of our company. I want you to make this the center of your framework for developing a winning team. Do so by *Setting the Example*: You show your soldiers every day what right looks like. Provide your platoon purpose, direction, and motivation. Give them feedback so they know, down to the soldier, that their hard work is accomplishing something and that they are going somewhere. Show them where they need to go and tell them when they get there.

3. The one soldier quality that soldiers care the most about in combat (besides courage) is competence. **DISCIPLINED** leaders seek to be more and more competent, mentally sharp, and technically and tactically proficient. You must be completely committed to learning the tools of your profession.

    a. Training. Concentrate on our METL and the critical tasks that support it. You need to understand our training management doctrine and how to plan and execute excellent training. Always begin with leader enabling training, include individual skill training, and then focus on our standard battle drills and critical collective tasks. Get your platoon ready to execute their wartime mission under all conditions.

    b. Maintaining. We can neither train nor execute our combat mission if we don't have operational equipment. I expect you to maintain your equipment. Know and report the correct status of your equipment and track deficiencies through the Army Maintenance System until they are fixed. Incorporate maintenance training into every maintenance period and hold your subordinate leaders accountable. Maintain 100% property accountability and ensure all property is properly hand receipted to the appropriate level.

    c. Safety. Understand and incorporate risk management/force protection into all training and operations. Always identify hazards and do everything you can to reduce risks. This is a way of thinking that boils down to doing the right thing and keeping our soldiers safe.

Reinforce safety during soldiers' off time, especially with regards to drinking and driving.

4. Be **PHYSICALLY FIT** and develop physically fit soldiers. Physical training is the most important training conducted on a daily basis; consider physical training as important as any METL-based training on the schedule. Our goal is to develop and maintain a challenging, fun, and progressive PT program that produces physically fit soldiers that can accomplish our mission. This area includes our day-to-day PT program, foot marches, health and welfare, sick call, and educating our soldiers on health and fitness issues. Finally, enjoy PT and help make it fun and challenging for all your soldiers.

5. Be a part of building a **MOTIVATED** outfit. Our goal is to develop a great command climate that is based on trust, respect, and true compassion for every soldier and family in the company. In short, let's develop a great unit that we are all proud of and enjoy being a part of.

    a.   In addition to always doing what you say you will do, leaders must demonstrate compassion and genuine respect for their subordinates in order to gain trust. Truly treating others the way you would want to be treated is the rule that should guide every leader's behavior.

    b.   Do everything you possibly can to take care of the soldiers entrusted to you and to make them feel like they are a significant part of our important mission. When it comes to things like counseling soldiers, writing their NCOERs, ensuring their pay problems get fixed, and awarding their PCS awards prior to their departure from the unit, always give 100%. Seek out opportunities to do and say things that will convince each individual that he is an essential part of a whole team—one that others depend upon to get their part done.

    c.   Another critical part of building a motivated and effective team is open communication. Ensure that every soldier knows what is on the training schedule and what is expected of him. No one should feel like they are "in the dark." Clearly and consistently explain your expectations and tell your soldiers how and why the unit's priorities are changing. In addition, know what is going on in your part of the unit. Provide feedback, but also seek it out. Excellent communication—up, down, and sideways—is fundamental to a motivated and effective unit.

d.   Finally, do not forget that in combat, mission accomplishment drives morale far more than the other way around, and the best way to take care of soldiers is to fully prepare them for tomorrow's battle. Let us then develop a warrior attitude with the will to win that begins with the will to *get ready* that is the hallmark of all great teams.

6. My door is open and I always have time for the soldiers of this company. One of my main goals is to help you grow as a leader, and I will spend time counseling, teaching, and mentoring you with the goal of making you and this company the best we can possibly be. Set the example in all things and remember that everything you do has an impact on the unit—when in doubt, **DO THE RIGHT THING!**

CHAPTER 2 -- DISCIPLINED

As we stated in the first chapter of this book, we believe winning combat teams are leader-powered, disciplined, fit, and motivated. Effective units have a culture marked by the willingness to pay the price to get ready and an almost fanatic dedication to learning and applying new knowledge. We chose the word discipline to describe this aspect of a winning team because the Latin root of the word means "to learn" and implies that disciplined units are learning units that pay the price required to develop skilled competence.

Training, maintenance, and safety are the three key components that make up the discipline "spoke" (remember the wheel metaphor? See page 20). In this chapter, we will talk about all three. Our goal is not to regurgitate doctrine but to share our perspective and to spark your thinking about these critical aspects of command. Although we have written this based on our light infantry backgrounds, this chapter is full of principles and techniques that are applicable to any company-level commander preparing his or her unit for combat.

Section 1. Training: Identify the "Big Rocks" and Plan, Plan, Plan

> Training is our priority—it is the cornerstone of combat readiness. Our nation expects us to prepare its sons for battle. To lose one soldier because he wasn't properly trained is dereliction of duty.
>
> – General Carl E. Vuono, former CSA

Simply put, training is the foundation of what we do. Preparing soldiers for combat is our sacred duty. Ralph Puckett underscores this when he says, "let no soul cry out, 'if only I had been properly trained.'"[44]

---

[44] Ralph Puckett, from a class he gave company commanders at Schofield Barracks, HI on 11 Jan 1996.

"Training management is the process used by Army leaders to identify training requirements and then plan, resource, execute and evaluate training... it is a continuous cycle of planning, executing, and assessing."[45] Because there are only 24 hours in a day, you first need to figure out what your unit's "big rocks" are in training—what you are expected to be able to do in combat. Second, you need to clarify these training priorities for your subordinate leaders, and establish effective training-management systems that help discipline you and your leaders as you seek to make quality training the norm in your unit. Only you can provide the emphasis necessary to make it happen. And like anything worthwhile, this is hard work.

In this section, we will focus primarily on prioritizing and planning training. We will give you some ideas on how to inspire all of your subordinate leaders to work together to prioritize and plan, and continually learn from their experience. We will conclude the section with some practical training tips.

Mission Essential Task List (METL)

Several items on your 90-day agenda should be your outfit's METL, Critical Collective Tasks, and Critical Individual Tasks. Bottom line: What are the "big rocks" when it comes to training? General Bruce Clarke wrote:

> Do essential things first. There is not enough time for the commander to do everything. Each commander will have to determine wisely what is essential .... Nonessentials should not take up time required for essentials.[46]

The first step in this process, of course, is figuring out what the "essentials" are. Doctrine says that you develop your company METL, taking into account the battalion METL and your wartime mission, and present it to the battalion commander for approval.[47] Theoretically, each new company commander

---

[45] *TC 25-30 A Leader's Guide to Company Training Meetings*, April 1994.

[46] Bruce Clark as quoted in *FM 25-101 Battle Focused Training*, 1990: p. 2-1.

[47] See *FM 25-101 Battle Focused Training*, 1990: p. 2-7.

would go through the process of figuring out what the "essentials" are. This may appear inefficient, but it is incredibly effective and even essential to the company commander understanding the very basis for training management in his or her specific unit. However, your company METL more than likely will have already been developed, and probably has been dictated at brigade or even division level. However, we highly recommend that you review your company METL from the ground up and present your work to the battalion commander— even if he doesn't ask you to do so.

Where do you start? First, do your homework. Read up on the doctrine that describes METL development in FMs 25-100 and 25-101. Review your unit's purpose—why the unit exists— and most likely combat mission. Ask yourself what your higher headquarters expects you to be able to do in combat. Study the division, brigade, and battalion METL, and review the last battalion and brigade quarterly training briefs and training guidance. Talk to your battalion commander and S3, and get input from your fellow company commanders who have probably worked through this process once already. Collect any existing documents or information in the battalion or the company on METL and collective tasks, looking for matrices and T, P, U evaluations.

If your unit gets deployed on a contingency-type mission, you will want to go through the same process to analyze the new mission requirements and to focus your company training. Do not let your wartime METL define who you are as a unit. Embrace change and start getting your soldiers ready to accomplish the new mission. Two examples of deployments that may cause a significant shift in your training priorities include rotations to the Sinai or Kosovo. A wartime example from our past is Operation Desert Shield. Units spent months focusing their training on a specific mission, and they did not waste any time training on previous mission essential tasks that they were not going to execute (e.g., the 82nd Airborne Division conducted no airborne training for eight months). Finally, upon returning from long deployments you will need to refocus your unit on their "normal" training priorities.

We mentioned that company commanders usually are not required to present their METL to the battalion commander for approval because it is already a "done deal." Furthermore, little to no work is usually done on identifying what additional company collective tasks and platoon collective tasks are critical to accomplishing the company METL. FM 25-100 refers to a "Battle Task" as a subordinate unit METL task that is critical to the accomplishment of your METL task. Platoons don't have METL, but they certainly have collective tasks that must be trained if you expect to accomplish your company METL. We will call these "Critical Collective Tasks."

Platoon Critical Collective Tasks

Just like we think it is important for you to develop or at least thoroughly review your company training "essentials," we think it is just as important that you require your subordinate leaders to conduct a ground-up review of *their* training "essentials." You can achieve this by requiring them to figure out what the platoon critical collective tasks are in your unit. You want to develop a complete list; however, you want to keep the final list as short as humanly possible. Here is how to do it:

First, give a class to your subordinate leaders (PLs and PSGs) on the METL development process that lays the doctrinal foundation for them. A better technique is to assign portions to the PLs & PSGs—have them present the class, but you keep them on track. Discuss your wartime mission, battalion METL, and current company METL. Take a look at the last self-evaluation of your METL and critical collective tasks in terms of T, P, and U. Ensure every leader has a copy of both the company and platoon MTP for your unit. Walk them through the manuals and ensure they understand how the manuals define each collective task (do not assume this has been done before). Finish this session by giving them the following requirement:

Task. Develop a platoon critical collective task list

Condition. Given appropriate references (MTPs, drill books, FMs), a discussion with the CO about doctrine and current company METL, and sufficient time, platoon leaders will work with their subordinate leaders to generate a list of platoon collective tasks.

Standard. A list of platoon tasks that must be trained in order for the company to execute its METL to standard.

Following this discussion that gives them the doctrine and their current METL/critical collective task list, give them a couple of days to crack open their MTPs, drill books, and the minds of their subordinate leaders. You have already created energy focused on training the unit because you have the leaders evaluating what tasks are most important, reading the manuals to see exactly how doctrine defines the task, and talking about it with their subordinates. This will be the first time some of your leaders will have been made aware of their unit's METL and critical collective tasks and (oh, by the way) how to find them in the manual.

Now, bring your leaders back together and let them lay out what they think should be the platoon critical collective tasks that support the company METL. You want as short a list as possible that will allow you to focus your limited training time and resources. Figure out what the common ground is and discuss the differences, allowing each leader to explain why one task should have priority over another. If you can't decide on the last couple, adjourn the meeting and let it lie for a couple of days before you come back together and, ideally, arrive at a consensus. Remember that, in addition to gaining a clear training focus, you are also seeking to foster a deeper sense of responsibility in your subordinate leaders for their training. That is why you want to go through this process even if you already have a list of platoon critical collective tasks in the company.

End State: You have a platoon critical collective task list in writing that tells your outfit the most important things to train on. Your leaders understand training in a new light, they have a clear training focus, and they feel ownership for the company METL. Even if you come up with the same list that already existed, you have a new knowledge and understanding that did not exist before.

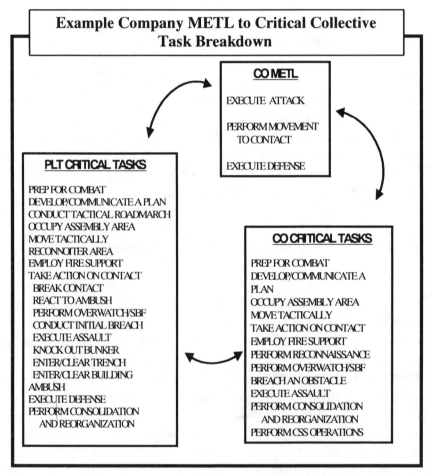

Example Company METL to Critical Collective Task Breakdown

CO METL

EXECUTE ATTACK

PERFORM MOVEMENT TO CONTACT

EXECUTE DEFENSE

PLT CRITICAL TASKS

PREP FOR COMBAT
DEVELOP/COMMUNICATE A PLAN
CONDUCT TACTICAL ROADMARCH
OCCUPY ASSEMBLY AREA
MOVE TACTICALLY
RECONNOITER AREA
EMPLOY FIRE SUPPORT
TAKE ACTION ON CONTACT
 BREAK CONTACT
 REACT TO AMBUSH
 PERFORM OVERWATCH/SBF
 CONDUCT INITIAL BREACH
EXECUTE ASSAULT
 KNOCK OUT BUNKER
 ENTER/CLEAR TRENCH
 ENTER/CLEAR BUILDING
AMBUSH
EXECUTE DEFENSE
PERFORM CONSOLIDATION
 AND REORGANIZATION

CO CRITICAL TASKS

PREP FOR COMBAT
DEVELOP/COMMUNICATE A PLAN
OCCUPY ASSEMBLY AREA
MOVE TACTICALLY
TAKE ACTION ON CONTACT
EMPLOY FIRE SUPPORT
PERFORM RECONNAISSANCE
PERFORM OVERWATCH/SBF
BREACH AN OBSTACLE
EXECUTE ASSAULT
PERFORM CONSOLIDATION
 AND REORGANIZATION
PERFORM CSS OPERATIONS

Finish this process by creating an evaluation worksheet that lists the collective tasks, and have your subordinate leaders identify where they are in terms of T, P, and U on each of them. Re-evaluate this assessment monthly or after each task is trained.

We value leaders who achieve results. This technique will help hold your leaders accountable for achieving results in training.

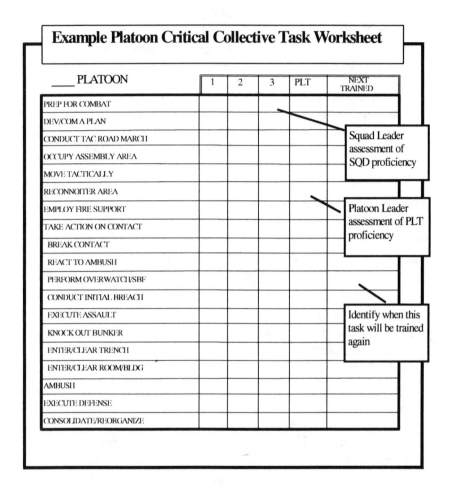

Make sure that you talk with your leaders about what T, P, and U actually mean. TC 25-30 lays this out well:[48]

---

[48] *TC 25-30 A Leader's Guide to Company Training Meetings*, 1994: Figure 3-1.

Proficiency in terms of T, P, U:

T= "Trained" The unit can perform the task to standard without any significant shortcomings. Train to maintain proficiency.
P= "Practice" The unit can perform task with some shortcomings. The shortcomings are not severe enough to require complete retraining.
U= "Untrained" The Unit cannot perform task to standard.

Critical Individual Tasks

The next step in this important process is to make the link between your critical collective tasks and the individual tasks that support them. Some people call this "walking the dog" on a collective task. Bottom line: In order to accomplish the collective task, you must be trained on the individual tasks that support it. (FM 25-101 describes the process of getting from collective tasks to individual tasks in chapter two).

Your unit will gain tremendous individual training focus if you identify the most critical individual soldier tasks that support your critical collective tasks. Some leaders find it helpful to list the individual tasks for each duty position in the company; however, we found it much more practical to simplify the final product so that it was an overall list of critical individual tasks for the company as a whole.[49]

One of your 1SG's main responsibilities is individual training for your company, so give him the ball in this area and let him, working with the NCOs, develop the list of individual soldier tasks that are critical to the overall success of your unit. Your goal is not to regurgitate the MTP or Soldier's Manual of Common Tasks, but to hone the hundreds of individual tasks found in your applicable MTP down to the most critical ones for your unit (there are 237 supporting skill level 1 tasks alone in ARTEP 7-8 MTP). By doing so, you focus your NCOs on what is most important in your unit.

---

[49] This is clearly dependent on what kind of unit you command and the diversity of individual MOSs within it.

Critical Individual Task List
(Light Infantry Company Example)

Camouflage self and individual equipment

Navigate from one point on the ground to another while
dismounted

Perform foot march (12 miles/4 hours)

Move as a member of a fire team

Perform movement techniques during MOUT

Move under direct fire

Engage targets with individual weapon

Construct individual fighting positions

Prepare a range card for a M240/M249 MG

Employ a M18A1 mine

Employ hand grenades

Prepare the M136 (AT-4) for firing

Report enemy information

Operate a PRC-119 and PRC-126

Send/receive a radio message

Operate PLUGGER

Operate individual night vision equipment

Evaluate a casualty

Treat a casualty

Your 1SG may decide to include this list of critical individual tasks in his NCOs' leader books. Team leaders now have a clear focus. Instead of being overwhelmed by the hundreds of tasks that their soldiers are supposed to be able to perform, they have a reasonable list of tasks that they know are critical to the success of the squad, platoon, and company. Team leaders can easily track the training proficiency of each of their soldiers on these tasks. When training opportunities arise (opportunity training, formerly known as hip-pocket training), they will know exactly which critical individual tasks to train on.

End State: You have a critical individual task list in writing that tells everyone in the outfit what the most critical individual tasks are. Once again, you have given your leaders a training focus, and have taught them how individual training fits into the overall training strategy of the unit. Training makes more sense to them now, and they already feel a sense of satisfaction that they never had before.

If, in fact, we must do essential things first, then we need to identify what the essential things are. The process of analyzing and determining these priorities will provide tremendous focus in your unit—this focus will drive training management and will be the foundation for your success in training.

Training-Management Systems

Immediately after assuming command, you will want to spend time with your leaders discussing the systems that are already in place to help you manage training. Just like we mentioned with METL, have a class with your PLs teaching different aspects of training management. Use FMs 25-100 and 25-101, your division 350-1, and your battalion training-management SOP as references. Boil down Army doctrine and your division and battalion SOP/guidance to one or two sheets of paper to help your leaders understand the training-management process in your unit. They must understand the timeline and standard for when you are required to have the company-training schedule turned in to battalion, and for requesting resources such as land, transportation, and ammunition.

Be an expert on your division training-management system and plan, plan, plan. Know exactly when the land and range management conferences are and never be caught by surprise. Don't let this one get by you, no matter how focused you are on the short term. A successful company commander is able to look beyond the *25-meter target* to what is coming up in the next six months to one year. Each division has different obstacles in this area. When we commanded in the 25th Infantry Division, because of all the joint users, the Land and Range Conference was usually ahead of the commander's quarterly training guidance (QTG). Because of this, we had to be ahead of battalion and, in some cases, brigade in our planning. You may face similar circumstances in your unit. Work hard to get your boss's intent for long-term training events and what he or she is going to put on the calendar so that you can work ahead of the land and range conference. **Without land and ammo it is hard to train**—you must be personally involved in this with your XO.

Leader Azimuth Check/Off-Site

The catalyst for effective training management is a quarterly azimuth check when you and your leaders take time to pause, reflect, plan the future, and have some fun. It is most effective when you take all your leaders to an off-site location away from distractions. Support cycle is the best time to run it—a Thursday night/Friday morning works well.[50] The azimuth check is the time when you re-look the unit vision, compare it with current reality, and plan the future. Conducting this review will unleash tremendous energy and will create a deep sense of team and purpose among your soldiers.

As you plan the off-site, select a location that provides a place to sleep and to meet. Camping can be both fun and inexpensive. A highlight for Nate was hiking and camping on the Na Pali Trail on the island of Kauai with his leaders. Bellows AFB seems to be the most appropriate location on Oahu because there is a conference room that comfortably supports meetings, and the campsite lends itself to an affordable overnight stay. Every post in the Army has an appropriate location close by—be creative and ask around.

The process begins before the off-site. Two weeks prior, publish the itinerary, provide something to read for an

---

[50] While the leadership is gone, have one of your squared-away sergeants run a junior-leader day in garrison where soldiers take over leadership positions within the company.

OPD/NCOPD, and hand out platoon Quarterly Leader Assessment (QLA) packets.[51]

Include a questionnaire for squad leaders and above; ask them to return it to you one week prior to the off-site. Questions like these work well:

- Are we accomplishing our vision?
- What are we doing currently that doesn't match up with our vision?
- What are three things that our company can do better?
- What are three things we are doing right and need to continue doing?
- What are the top three collective tasks/battle drills you feel we need to work this next quarter?
- What are the top five individual tasks we need to work this next quarter?
- What are two topics for OPD/NCOPD you feel we need to focus on?
- What is one thing that I can do to improve as your commander?
- What is one thing that you can improve on as a SL, PSG, or PL?

Require your platoon leaders to run a quarterly leader assessment (QLA) with their squad leaders. One week prior to the off-site, have the platoon leaders brief you using the slides that you gave them (do it with all of the platoon leaders together). In addition to their current status, ensure that the platoon leaders talk about upcoming training and how that training will affect their current training proficiency.

We also recommend that you treat your battalion commander's quarterly training guidance (QTG) as an operations order. During the week prior to the off-site, conduct a mission analysis of the QTG with your platoon leaders to identify all the

---

[51] The platoon QLA packets are slides that highlight the status of individual and collective training and of personnel issues such as manning and schools.

specified and implied tasks. Backbrief your battalion commander to ensure you clearly understand his intent.

Finally, collect and read through the questionnaires that your leaders filled out. Using butcher-block, write each question and the answers that were given for it using one sheet per question. Star the answers that come up more than once. Have your RTOs type up all of the sheets to be used as handouts during the off-site.

It is essential that you and your subordinate leaders spend some quality time planning the off-site. Having a planning checklist is essential to your success. Here is one that will help you as you plan your first off-site:

Example Off-Site Planning Checklist

T-8 ☐ Select dates and finalize location
☐ Complete draft itinerary
☐ Invite guest speaker if applicable
T-6 ☐ Forecast resource requirements (location, food, etc.)
☐ Finalize itinerary
T-2 ☐ Hand out: Professional development reading
    Blank QLA packets
    Questionnaires for squad leaders
    & above
T-1 ☐ Have platoon leaders brief QLAs
☐ Conduct mission analysis of battalion quarterly training guidance (QTG)
☐ Collect questionnaires and collate answers on butcher-block
☐ Have RTOs prepare butcher-block calendars for use on day 2 of off-site

---

There are probably a million different ways to conduct an off-site. In fact, you will find that each of your off-sites will be different depending on circumstances and the lessons you apply from the previous off-site AAR. The agenda below worked very well for us as a general SOP that we could adjust from.

Example Agenda
BBQ
Company Assessment
PT – Sporting Event
Current Reality vs. Vision
Professional Development
Plan Upcoming Training

After dinner on the first evening, pull everyone together to talk about the questionnaires that they filled out. The commander might start this time out by sharing with the group the personal feedback he received from the anonymous surveys. Nate's willingness to openly discuss the recommendations for his own improvement modeled how he wanted the entire team to respond to honest feedback, and it set the tone for the entire off-site. Don't be defensive and remember to thank your soldiers for their input.

Provide hard copies of the questionnaire summaries and post the butcher-block sheets that summarize the answers for each question. Use these summaries to generate discussion about what current reality is for the company. You want the leaders to take an honest and open look at how the unit is doing. Then talk about the company vision and core values—ensure that everyone understands and agrees with these. Finally, based on the differences between current reality and the vision, talk about what the company needs to change in order to reach the vision.

Establish the ground rules prior to the meeting. The meeting will be more successful if everyone agrees to be honest, to listen to others, and to not be defensive. As we stated earlier, your personal example up front will set the tone. After the first time, it will become easier and the "nay-sayers" will become supporters.

In fact, the biggest critics will usually become the biggest advocates after they see the benefits first hand.

The next morning, do PT with everyone. Two ideas that work well include platoon-on-platoon competitions, and competitions between officers and NCOs (football, soccer, tug-of-war, king-of-the-ring, volleyball, etc.). Whatever you choose, it should be fun and physically demanding.

Following breakfast, begin with an OPD. There are many techniques here. You can make it a dialogue based on the reading you handed out two weeks prior, or you may want to share something you personally have been learning about leadership. You might invite a guest speaker (e.g., a combat veteran) to share some experiences or personal insight. Whatever you do, you want the meeting to be thought provoking and inspiring, and to create an open atmosphere.

Following the OPD, flow into planning. This is the meat of the off-site and will last three to four hours with a lunch break in the middle. The final product will be a training calendar (probably an 80% solution) and a matrix that clearly delineates responsibility and the suspense for each key training event the company will execute.

A great way to begin the planning phase is for you to provide the group an overview of the major training events that are six to eighteen months out. Then have your platoon leaders brief the mission analysis of the battalion QTG, the overall current company training assessment (based on the platoon QLAs), and review 350-1 training requirements. At this point, all your leaders understand what is coming up down the road, they understand the current training status of the unit, and they have an understanding of dictated and required training for the upcoming quarter. Now, using this information and the information that came out of the meeting the night before, make a list of all the training events you are required to or want to conduct during the upcoming quarter. Put these events on large post-it notes, one per note.[52]

---

[52] Also hang on the wall the butcher-block sheets from the meeting the night before and refer to them at the end of the planning session to ensure you fixed what needed fixing and maintained what needed to be maintained. This

Prior to the meeting, create calendars on sheets of butcher block that already have known training events written in.[53] Hang these calendars up on the walls around the room. Then, using the large post-it notes, begin posting the training events on the calendar. Using the post-it notes allows you to move training around and shows the participants that you are flexible.

The company XO and commodity chiefs should work resource requests as the planning process progresses. Don't get bogged down in details—lay out on butcher-block the basic concept for each key training event and then assign it to a specific platoon. That platoon leader is then responsible for the event and will write an MOI that is due in draft form at week T-8.

As an example, squad STX lanes may be one of the key training events you decide to conduct during the upcoming quarter. You choose the specific tasks to focus on during the STX lanes based on your training assessment and also based on what other key training events are coming up in the future. Post the yellow sticky on the calendar so that everyone sees where that training is going to happen. Use a butcher-block to outline the initial concept for the STX lanes and then assign a specific platoon that will be responsible for the details. As mentioned earlier, the platoon leader owes a draft MOI for the event at T-8.

In addition to key training events, you want to designate a date, outline an initial concept, and assign responsibility for the other events going on during the upcoming quarter. Things like marksmanship ranges, OPD/NCOPDs, command maintenance, inventories, company PT, FRG events, company parties, and even BOSS trips might be examples of events you can plan. One extremely effective technique is to divide into smaller teams to work these events. A checklist of events to accomplish each quarter (based on 350-1 and unit goals) will help ensure that you

---

method ensures that your planning is tied directly into your vision and core values.

[53] It is critical that you get with the battalion commander/S3 prior to the off-site, and ensure that you have all the battalion dictated training represented on this calendar. The more you communicate with your boss, the more you will minimize frustration following the off-site.

don't forget anything (See training-requirements checklist example on page 79).

You might have one team, for example, designated to plan the general company PT plan for the upcoming quarter. The XO might lead another team that lays out the command maintenance plan for the upcoming quarter. Another team might focus on professional development and leader training. This should always be done after you have completed the key training events so that these teams plan in the context of what is happening on the calendar. You and the 1SG provide each team with initial guidance and then "float" around and listen to what is going on. When the teams are finished, reconvene the entire group and have each team brief what they came up with.

Another sheet you want hanging on the wall during the meeting is a task matrix that rolls up who is responsible for the key training events, when the draft MOI is due, and any other suspenses or due outs that come up during the meeting (See example below). If you take an RTO or training NCO/clerk with you, he or she can input the calendar and task matrix into the computer so that, by the end of the off-site, you have a good product. You depart the off-site with a working calendar, initial concepts for every key event occurring during the upcoming quarter, and a matrix that lays out suspenses and fixes responsibility.

Example Task Responsibility Matrix				
Task/ Event	Execution Date(s)	OIC/ NCOIC	Initial Concept Brief (DTG)	MOI Due (T-8)

Your team will leave this meeting feeling that they own the plan—they will say, "It is our plan, and we know where we need to head to ensure the company is successful in executing it!"

Before you end the off-site, take time to summarize what was accomplished, and again draw attention to the vision and core values. Explain that there is never a perfect plan and that change is inevitable. However, regardless of how much the calendar changes, you and your leaders will see how important the 1 ½ day event was. The rest of training management will flow naturally out of the off-site. We have heard many people ask why they should bother planning if everything just changes anyway. Our experience is that the further out and more detailed we planned, the more likely we were to actually do the training. What is the alternative to this kind of team-planning concept? Well, it is you, the XO, and 1SG working twice as hard, few of your subordinates understanding the big picture, and a training plan that is driven by forces outside of your company.

Training-Requirements Checklist

An invaluable tool to help you plan training is a "required-training checklist." Below is an example of a partial checklist that will give you an idea of what we are talking about. Scrub your division 350-1 and your battalion and brigade-level training requirements to make sure your version of this matrix is complete. Although you may very well choose not to do everything on the list based on time available and your own priorities, having a matrix like this will prevent you from simply forgetting required training. In addition, it will help you and your subordinates project future training.

Example Training-Requirements Checklist (extract from a 25th ID(L) rifle company)					
Task	**Standard**		**Last**	**Next**	**Next**
METL/Collective Tng	**350-1**	**GOAL** (if different)			
SQD LFX	Q (PLT COUNTS)				
SQD EXEVAL	A (24hrs min)				
WPN Training/Qual					
M4	S	M			
M203	S				
Individual Tng					
Call For Fire (TSFO)	N/A	Q			
Land Navigation	N/A	Q			
PT					
4 mi Run	M	W			
APFT/Silver Streamer	S/A				
CLASSES					
Water Safety Brief	A				
Risk Ass./Safety Class	S(NCOs)				
NCOPD/OPD	M				
Legend: A = 1x year; S = 2x year; T = 3x year; M = 1x month; W = 1x week					

"Rolling T" Planning Method

Develop a system to manage your planning cycle that works for you and your leaders. Nate found the "Rolling T" to be the most effective method. It requires three large dry erase boards that have four weeks laid out permanently on each of them. Ensure that you have a margin on the left and room for notes each week on the right. Then lay out the calendar from   T-0 (current training week) to T-11 in dry erase. Write the month, fiscal week number (i.e., 1 to 52), and what "T-week" it is (e.g., T-2) in the left margin. In the "Remarks" section on the right, put what training cycle you are in for that week. Then write in all the main training events. [54]   You will want to establish a regular

---

[54] Nate got this idea from Ted Johnson, his predecessor in command of A/2-5 IN at Schofield Barracks, HI.

time when you personally work on training management. Fridays usually work best, depending on when your training meeting is.

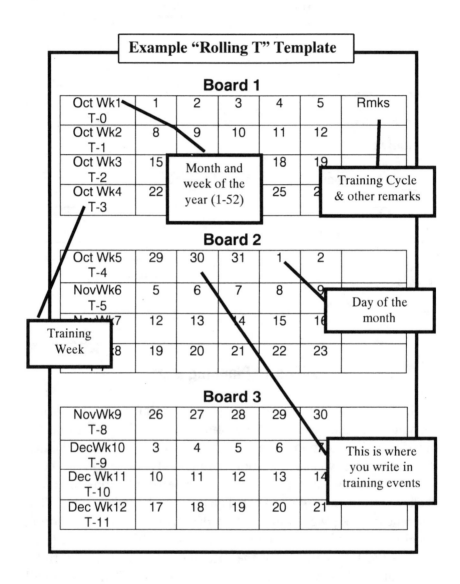

Example "Rolling T" Template

Board 1

Oct Wk1 T-0	1	2	3	4	5	Rmks
Oct Wk2 T-1	8	9	10	11	12	
Oct Wk3 T-2	15			18	19	
Oct Wk4 T-3	22			25	2	

Month and week of the year (1-52)

Training Cycle & other remarks

Board 2

Oct Wk5 T-4	29	30	31	1	2	
NovWk6 T-5	5	6	7	8	9	
NovWk7	12	13	14	15	16	
8	19	20	21	22	23	

Day of the month

Training Week

Board 3

NovWk9 T-8	26	27	28	29	30	
DecWk10 T-9	3	4	5	6	7	
Dec Wk11 T-10	10	11	12	13	14	
Dec Wk12 T-11	17	18	19	20	21	

This is where you write in training events

A blow up of the first week, including the main training events, might look like this:

Oct	1	2	3	4	5	Rmks
Wk 1 T-0	Maint. Tng Mtg	M-16 PMI	M16 Qualification Range 1, 2		Recovery AAR	DRF 3 Green Cycle

It is the first week of the year and is the current training week (T-0). The battalion is on DRF-3 and is in a Green Training Cycle status. Finally, the main training event for the week is M-16 qualification.

Let's work through an example. Imagine that it is 5 October and you just completed the week of training from the above example. You are preparing for your next training meeting, which will occur on Monday, 8 October. Go to your "Rolling T" boards and erase the current T-0 (the week you just completed), and write T-11 in its place. In this example, T-11 is Week 13 which happens to be 24-28 December (Happy Holidays!). You are in support cycle. Write in the main training events for that week.

Then change *all* the "T" weeks (down the left margin) by subtracting one (e.g., T-1 becomes T-0).

This can be a bit confusing at first, but it is by far the best method. It forces you to think in terms of training weeks and will keep your training management on track. This process continues each week by merely erasing the T-0 week and in its place putting the new T-11 and then subtracting 1 from each "T" week.

One interesting thing that happens is that as each new quarter begins, all the week numbers are lined up in order again, helping you and your leaders to see a quarterly pattern. During your quarterly off-site, you focus on the entire upcoming quarter, while at the weekly training meeting you will focus on weeks T-8 to T-0.

Example Template for 8 October Tng Mtg

Board 1

Dec Wk13 T-11	24	25	26	27	28	Support
Oct Wk2 T-0	8	9	10	11		
Oct Wk3 T-1	15	Erase Wk 1 & add Wk 13 which is T-11		18		
Oct Wk4 T-2	22			25		

Board 2

Oct Wk5 T-3	29	30	31	1
Nov Wk 6 T-4	5	6	7	8
Nov Wk7 T-5	12	13	14	15
Update all training week numbers	19	20	21	22

Board 3

Nov Wk9 T-7	26	27	28	29	
Dec Wk10 T-8	3	4	5	6	7
Dec Wk11 T-9	10	11	12	13	14
Dec Wk12 T-10	17	18	19	20	21

Note: After the initial setup, you replace the old T-0 with a new T-11 each week. It takes very little time and works perfectly with the Army's training management doctrine.

Training Meeting

There are many different ways to run a company training meeting.[55] However, there are several things that must happen for the meeting to be a success. First, there must be open dialogue about the past week's training. Recommendations on how to do things better "next time" must be captured and incorporated into future training. If this isn't happening, the entire process is corrupted. Second, based on the previous

---

[55] The best reference is *TC 25-30 A Leader's Guide To Company Training Meetings*, 1994.

week's training, your leaders need to evaluate their element's training proficiency. This evaluation holds them accountable for results, provides an assessment of current reality, and will guide you when planning future training. Third, at a minimum, you and your leaders must finalize the week of training that is due to battalion for signature.

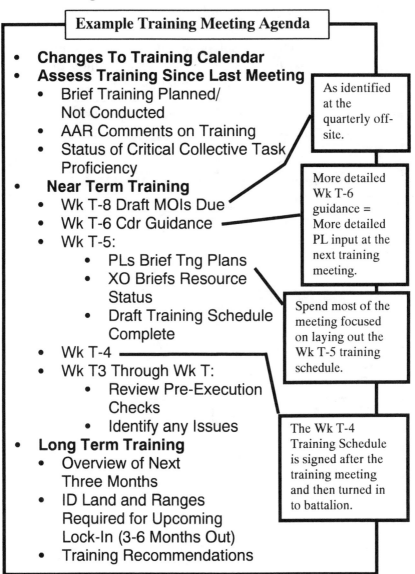

Example Training Meeting Agenda

- **Changes To Training Calendar**
- **Assess Training Since Last Meeting**
    - Brief Training Planned/ Not Conducted
    - AAR Comments on Training
    - Status of Critical Collective Task Proficiency

    > As identified at the quarterly off-site.

- **Near Term Training**
    - Wk T-8 Draft MOIs Due
    - Wk T-6 Cdr Guidance
    - Wk T-5:
        - PLs Brief Tng Plans
        - XO Briefs Resource Status
        - Draft Training Schedule Complete
    - Wk T-4
    - Wk T3 Through Wk T:
        - Review Pre-Execution Checks
        - Identify any Issues

    > More detailed Wk T-6 guidance = More detailed PL input at the next training meeting.

    > Spend most of the meeting focused on laying out the Wk T-5 training schedule.

- **Long Term Training**
    - Overview of Next Three Months
    - ID Land and Ranges Required for Upcoming Lock-In (3-6 Months Out)
    - Training Recommendations

    > The Wk T-4 Training Schedule is signed after the training meeting and then turned in to battalion.

We found that using a fill-in-the-blank training meeting worksheet was essential to an effective training meeting. Use the example below (based on TC 25-30) or download the examples on www.CompanyCommand.com. Spend some time prior to the meeting filling in the left side, and leave the right side blank for your subordinate leaders to make notes during the meeting. The worksheet should be set up to follow your agenda and therefore will help keep you on track. Moreover, it will put the meeting attendees on the same sheet of music during the meeting. It is extremely beneficial to have a record of your training meetings, so file your copies in a training meeting binder.

Example Training Meeting Worksheet	
8 OCT 01	**Training Meeting**
DATE	
FOCUS ITEM/AGENDA	**TNG MTG NOTES**
Assess Tng Since Last MTG	
T-8 Draft MOIs Due (3-7 DEC):	
T-6 Cdr's Guidance (19-23 NOV):	
T-5 (12-16 NOV): Dry Erase Board	

This is the key week for your training meeting

Based on our experience, the bulk of the time in the training meeting should be spent on Week T-5. Lay the week out on a dry erase board prior to the meeting. During the meeting, get into the details to include key times such as weapons draw and meal times. This will become your training contract with your soldiers and your boss, so you want to get it right. Soliciting input on Week T-5 at the training meeting will make a tremendous difference and will lead to quality training schedules that are actually used by your soldiers.

Command-and-Staff Meeting Side-Bar

There are three meetings that must be conducted on a weekly basis in your unit. We have already discussed the training meeting and will discuss the training-resource meeting next. The third meeting you need to have is a meeting focused on administrative and personnel issues that some people call the command-and-staff meeting. We mention it here because we highly encourage you not to roll it into your training meeting. Doing so will take away from the clear training focus that is required for your training meeting to be effective. Here are two recommendations for accomplishing this: One technique is to break for five minutes after the training meeting and then reconvene for the command and staff. Another technique is to do it during your morning leader huddle.

We had leader huddles every morning before PT while in garrison. On Mondays we quickly previewed the upcoming week, and on Fridays we covered command-and-staff issues.

If you and your leaders are properly prepared, the command-and-staff meeting can be completed in fifteen minutes. Doing this meeting on Friday mornings prevented us from having to take valuable time during the day for another meeting, and it also ensured that we were prepared for the battalion command-and-staff meeting that happened on Fridays in our battalions.

```
┌─────────────────────────────────────────────┐
│        Example Command-and-Staff             │
│             Meeting Agenda                    │
├─────────────────────────────────────────────┤
│                                               │
│  ┌──────────────────┐  ┌───────────────────┐ │
│  │ XO               │  │ 1SG               │ │
│  │ Award Status     │  │ Schools, Promotions│ │
│  │ OERs             │  │ NCOERs            │ │
│  │ 2406/Maint. Issues│ │ UCMJ/Chapter Status│ │
│  │                  │  │ Flags/Bars        │ │
│  │ PLs              │  │ Pay Problems      │ │
│  │ Re-enlistment    │  │ 30/60/90 Day Losses│ │
│  │ RIP Candidates   │  │                   │ │
│  │ Profile Status   │  │ CDR               │ │
│  │                  │  │ Bn Issues & Guidance│ │
│  │                  │  │ Cdr Comments      │ │
│  └──────────────────┘  └───────────────────┘ │
└─────────────────────────────────────────────┘
```

Training Schedule [56]

One of your RTOs must be trained on SATS with the ability to extract the draft T-6 training schedule off of the boards ("Rolling T"). **Do not get caught in the trap of writing your own training schedules!** If the training meeting is done properly, your RTO will easily be able to write up the draft training schedule one week prior to it being due to battalion. This will allow time for all your leaders to review it. Once you sign it, it becomes a contract that every key member of the outfit has agreed to.

The company training schedule is the most important document that you routinely produce. It is written for your unit, and not for someone at higher echelons; for it to have meaning, it must accurately reflect what is *actually* going to happen. Soldiers in the company should be able to look at the schedule and know what they are going to be doing. It must fix responsibility in terms of who is to be trained, by whom, and to what standard. This document flows from an effective training

---

[56] Many of the ideas in this section are taken directly from notes and comments made by Gary D. Speer to his subordinates while he commanded 3d Brigade, 25th ID(L) at Schofield Barracks, HI, 1994-1996.

meeting and is a clear sign of whether or not the unit is conducting effective training management. You and your leaders can either invest time up front in the training meeting and have a clear understanding of what is going to happen, or you can pull it out last minute and have a climate characterized by frustration and wasted time.

Suggestions for training schedules:

- **WHEN** – Self-explanatory. Be flexible about this during the Wk T-5 training meeting, but not once you have signed the training schedule. Force your leaders to think ahead and be realistic. If you hold them to this, training timelines will work; if you continually change times, your leaders will never have the discipline to think ahead. If MOIs are written in sufficient detail, the training schedule can reflect, "See MOI for detailed timeline." Turn the MOI in to battalion with the training schedule.

- **WHO** – Be as specific as possible. For example, the Co(-) can only be doing one thing at a time. Use selected personnel only when nothing else fits. Remember, if soldiers are confused when they read it, it is not sufficiently detailed.

- **WHAT** – Clearly ID "what" is being conducted, i.e. the task or mission. "NCOPD" is not nearly as good as "NCOPD – Rifle Marksmanship." Instead of just "FTX," include the METL task being trained. "M-16 Range" doesn't specify what the mission is—"M-16 Qualification" does.

- **WHERE** – Be specific.

- **TRAINER** – Clearly identify who is conducting the training, not who is holding the first formation. Identify by position or name whenever applicable. Being disciplined in this area will provide leaders the time necessary to prepare for training.

- **REFERENCE** – Reflect the task number where standards can be found. For individual training, this will almost always be the Soldiers Manual or EIB Pamphlet. For collective training, it will almost always be found in the appropriate MTP. There are exceptions where AR, FM, MOI, etc. apply. Unit SOP as a reference is often a cop-out. If you use this, we recommend including a copy of that section of your SOP. Do not assume that everyone knows the SOP or that the SOP applies exactly in the particular situation.

- **REMARKS** – Use for amplification. If you need to, add additional pages of notes to clarify for your soldiers what is going to happen.

Training-Resource Meeting

Properly resourcing training is essential to effective training management. Your XO will be in charge of resourcing and should use a resource matrix and a weekly training-resource meeting to help manage it. The matrix should be by event and "T week", and must include all classes of supply and support information (MILES, transpo, targets, ammo, medical, etc.). The weekly training-resource meeting should be run by your XO and attended by the 1SG, PSGs, commodity chiefs, and the armorer. It is the team's opportunity to ensure that all support is coordinated properly. This meeting complements the weekly training meeting and prevents the training meeting from becoming mired in support details.

Example Training-Resource Matrix								
Resource	Mon	Tue	Wed	Thur	Fri	Sat	Sun	Rmks
Class I								
Class III								
Class IV								
Etc.								

Although training support is primarily the XO's responsibility, she cannot do this successfully unless you are doing your job. She will only be effective if you are planning company training far enough out and forcing the platoons to properly forecast their required resources. Finally, you must be personally involved when it comes to ammunition and land, without which all your hard work and detailed planning might be for naught.

Training Ideas and Tips

We love talking about training, and often found ourselves hanging out on the porch (or lanai as they call it in Hawaii) talking about how to get the most out of training. Below, you will find some of the techniques that worked well for us. Our desire is that your thinking will be sparked and you will be able to use a few tips as you command your outfit. We also challenge you to get on www.CompanyCommand.com and begin sharing your own tips and lessons learned on training at the company level.

Before you read our tips, we would like to emphasize that the Army has provided us some great training doctrine. Use the eight-step training model and the principles of training outlined in FM 25-100 and FM 25-101 as you plan and execute your training.[57]

8-Step Training Model
1. **Plan the training**
2. **Train and certify leaders**
3. **Recon the site**
4. **Issue the plan**
5. **Rehearse and conduct PCIs**
6. **Execute**
7. **Conduct AARs**
8. **Retrain**

---

[57] Chapter 1 of FM 25-100, "Training The Force," is a must read. Several units have added two steps to the "8-Step" training model, thus making it a 10-Step" model: 1. Select the training objectives... and 10. Recover.

---

9 Principles of Training

1. Train as a combined arms team
2. Train as you fight
3. Use appropriate doctrine
4. Use performance-oriented training
5. Train to challenge
6. Train to sustain proficiency
7. Train using multi-echelon techniques
8. Train to maintain
9. Make cdrs the primary trainers

Suggestions for training:

• **Train using multi-echelon techniques whenever possible.**

First, think about where your training focus will be. We believe that squads are the building blocks for the success of the company, and that company commanders are responsible for training them. Therefore, we recommend that you consciously decide to focus your training at the squad level.

Second, think about how you can maximize your training opportunities. You can do this by planning multi-echelon training. While evaluating two levels down, you make the most of training when you train one level down. For example, think about conducting squad evaluations with platoon leaders and platoon sergeants participating. Imagine a platoon area ambush in which the squads are being evaluated yet the platoon leader and platoon sergeant are also participating in the training, in a command-and-control role. You might get some observer-controller (OC) help from outside your company, or you might rotate the training to allow PLs and PSGs from the other platoons to OC. Time is a premium. A multi-echelon training focus makes the most of your time, and it results in a more combat-ready unit.

- **Train individual and leader tasks before collective tasks.**

Leaders must ensure that their soldiers are trained on the individual tasks that support the collective tasks that are going to be trained, and they must do so prior to the collective training event. Create a climate in your unit where this happens without leaders having to be told. If your unit is going to incorporate claymores during an upcoming live-fire exercise, then squad leaders should automatically be drilling their soldiers on claymore emplacement, so that they can do it to standard under all conditions. If enter/clear a trench is the collective task, then a good squad leader will break that down and drill the squad on all the supporting pieces—from entering the trench under all conditions (day and night), to movement in the trench, to clearing corners, etc. This detailed training is not optional—it must happen, and you must ensure that time is given to junior leaders to execute this! How many times did John Elway practice taking a snap before the game, even though he had done so a million times before? The fundamentals must be reviewed before executing each collective task.

- **Use video during training—it is a powerful AAR tool.**

Videotape your training, and use the videos at your AARs. Instead of telling a soldier what he did, show him. At night, if you hold NVDs up to your video camera, you'll get a great picture. Your RTOs can do this for you. For every key training event get a generator, tent, light set, and TV, and your AARs will be much more effective. Examples: Videotape the blank fire exercise of a MOUT training event before the live fire from inside the room to show soldiers clearly if they hit and collapsed their sectors; video the ambush line after it is set in to show camouflage effectiveness; or video movement, especially at night. The ideas are limitless, but video is too often overlooked. Think about how much learning happens when a football team watches game tapes over and over again. The same level of learning can take place in a rifle company (or whatever unit you are in). Finally, keep the videos because they then become part of your leader-training package for future training.

- **Create healthy competition to breed excellence.**

Run key weapon system *top gun* competitions (events might include march and shoot, range card, assembly/disassembly, written test, crew drills through an obstacle course, etc.). A great technique for testing range cards is to have them do it on a range. Once the card is completed, hang cheesecloth in front of the gun and bring up targets. The AG will have to call out the targets as they come up—the gunner will make the adjustments from the range card and fire without seeing the target. Encourage Battalion to run a similar *top gun* competition with the company mortar sections.

- **Always work casualty evacuation.**

The more realistic you are, the better off your unit will be. Include having combat lifesavers administer IVs to assessed casualties during training. Doing so on live-fire exercises or foot marches is a realistic challenge that will pay huge dividends in combat.

- **Work the orders process at every opportunity—even when planning tactical foot marches.**

- **Work very hard to ensure your live-fire exercises are as realistic as possible.**

Any range constraints should be briefed simply as a constraint in the tactical scenario. For example, if a unit can't move through a certain area, then brief that area as a complex minefield. If you can't fire outside a certain area, then build into the scenario a friendly unit to your flank, etc. Be creative and use range constraints to help train your leaders. We know that the operations that we will be involved in will certainly include constraints. Also, leave safety to the executing chain of command as much as possible rather than putting the responsibility for safety completely on the range safety officer.

- **Include realistic force-on-force training.**

Too much focus on live fires can limit the range of experience your young leaders need—junior leaders' ability to think and react to a thinking enemy will not always be gained during live fires. A "live" OPFOR brings uncertainty and adversity that soldiers must be trained to handle. Just one example of incorporating this concept into your routine training is having OPFOR ambush your unit during foot marches so soldiers are trained to stay alert during movement.

- **Train marksmanship—we don't train it enough!**

Do not focus your unit on qualification, but rather on a quality marksmanship program focused on training your soldiers to kill the enemy under all conditions. Adapt this approach with all your weapon systems, not just your M16s. Simply put, if we can't hit what we shoot at, we will not be successful and we will die.

When you qualify M-16/M-4s, make it a first-class, multiple-day event. Although there are several ways to skin this cat, one great technique is to allocate the first day to nothing but preliminary marksmanship instruction (PMI). Allocate day two for zeroing, conducting known distance, practice record, and night firing.[58] Finally, on day three, conduct record qualification fire.

A combat focus will drive you to go beyond simply training for qualification. For example, under combat conditions we won't be in the prone on a sterile range. Therefore, work the

---

[58] The KD range gives soldiers direct feedback on where they are hitting the target. However, the Army has done away with most KD ranges. In the 25th ID(L), Puuloa Range by Barbers Point is the only KD range on the island—the Marines own it but have an agreement with the Army.

alternate firing positions. In addition, work reflexive firing using FM 90-10-1 as a guide. Moreover, make every night fire a quality training event that includes the use of all available night vision devices. Don't "finger drill" marksmanship training.

Schedule an M16 zero and qualification range every month. You will always have new soldiers that need to qualify, and it's an excellent way to continue your marksmanship focus. Even if there are only a few soldiers during support cycle who can get out to the range, their training will pay big dividends. Marksmanship is an individual task that supports everything we do—it must be a focus area for your unit.

- **Foot march in from every training event you have.**

If it is too far, foot march to the trucks or aviation assets. Be consistent—when your soldiers know this is the standard, it will not be an issue. (This is written from the "light" perspective.)

- **Train with the equipment that you will fight with.**

Be innovative and train your soldiers the way they will actually fight. For example, fill mortar cases with sand or cement and carry the rounds whenever you train as a company. Carry training hand grenades during training. Train with M203s whenever possible—at a minimum have team leaders go through the fire commands.

- **Constantly test and challenge your LTs tactically.**

You must develop bold, capable leaders who understand initiative within intent and are calm under intense pressure. Allow your unit to fail in training so you can see how leaders and soldiers react. Encourage your lieutenants to challenge you, too!

- **Incorporate indirect fires into everything you do.**

Your FSO needs to be at every training meeting you have, and the FSO's team needs to be out in the field every time you are. Also, bring your FSO and FSNCO to your leader off-sites and social events.

- **Use support cycle to train key skills.**

During support cycle, work hard to fence your mortars and M240 gunners from taskings, and get the resources for them to conduct a week of focused training. Also, support cycle is a great time to fence your AT teams from taskings and train them. Quality support is definitely the priority, but usually, especially if your 1SG is working with the other company 1SGs and the CSM, you can make this happen. It's a team effort across the battalion. Don't miss this opportunity! If possible, based on your taskings, you may be able to fence a platoon a week for training during support cycle. **Be very careful, though, not to load too much on the plate.** You and your leadership team must know instinctively how hard to push your unit and when you need to slow it down and let your soldiers relax—support cycle in many ways provides you that opportunity.

- **Finally, seek to earn any streamers or special designations available in your battalion or division.**

The 25th ID(L) offered streamers for excellence in PT, EIBs, and marksmanship. They are a great way to build pride in your unit, and they are achievable. Lay out the goal, achieve it, and morale will skyrocket! Your soldiers will know they are a part of something special.

Section 2. Maintenance

Maintaining takes on several dimensions for the soldier. It is his responsibility to assure his performance is not hindered by equipment failure. **It is his commander's responsibility to provide the time, materiel, and training to allow him to maintain his equipment.** And, it is the Army's responsibility to provide him the best "tools of the trade" that technology can offer.
    – General John A. Wickham, Jr., former CSA

Change-of-Command Inventory

Prior to your initial inventory, take time to talk to the battalion S-4, the battalion maintenance officer, and your executive officer. In addition to assessing the status of maintenance in your company, you want to learn the nuts and bolts of the maintenance SOP for both your company and your battalion. Look at your company's 2406 and have the XO talk you through what system is in place to manage and track non-mission-capable (NMC) equipment.

Use your change-of-command inventory to establish the priority that you place on accountability and maintenance. One thing that will help you immensely is having your supply sergeant make a book for you with copies of all the TMs for every piece of equipment you own. This book will make all the difference for you during the inventory itself and will continue to be beneficial throughout your command. Additionally, before the change-of-command inventory, have the supply sergeant prepare all sub-hand receipts and a spreadsheet for each of your hand receipts (PBO, OMA, and installation) such as the following example:[59]

---

[59] This idea came from Brian Prosser, Nate's battalion XO in 2-5 IN.

Example Property Accountability Sub-Hand Receipt Matrix				
Property Line	**Sub HR #1**	**Sub HR #2**	**Sub HR #3 (Armorer)**	**Cdr HR Total**
AB111 Work Gloves	2	2	0	4
XXXX M16	0	0	82	82
Etc.				

Include who the sub-hand receipt holder is.

Make sure your supply sergeant keeps this spreadsheet updated for you throughout your command. It will make it much easier to track the property in your unit.

All equipment on your hand receipt should be reflected on one of your sub-hand receipts. Additionally, the fewer sub-hand receipts you maintain, the easier it will be to track and account for your equipment. Lieutenants should sign for their platoon equipment from you so that they grow to understand this process. They are responsible for everything in their respective platoons, and getting them involved in equipment accountability is essential for their development.

During the change-of-command inventory process, make note of your observations and create a list of any areas that need improvement. This could range from equipment that needs to be fixed or ordered to areas that need to be cleaned up and better organized. During your initial counseling sessions with your 1SG and XO, give them this list and ask them to prioritize and immediately begin fixing what they can. Your fresh, critical eye will provide energy to areas that may have been overlooked and accepted over time. We recommend that you pay special attention to storage areas like lockers and closets that often become rats' nests—your attention early on will prevent problems later. Continue to refer to and update this list of deficiencies on a monthly basis when you do monthly inventories and sign your PBO hand-receipts.[60]

Command Maintenance and Training

We recommend that while in garrison your command maintenance day (typically Mondays) be the XO's training day. Charge your XO with developing a long-term plan that ensures 100% of the unit's equipment is properly maintained, and have the XO brief maintenance during training meetings just like the PLs brief platoon training.

Maintenance is training—period. Your soldiers must be trained on how to care for and maintain their equipment. Cleanliness is only part of this. Begin every command maintenance day with a hands-on maintenance class focused on a selected piece of equipment. Bring in maintenance experts from the division and battalion to share their expertise with your soldiers, and require that the appropriate –10s be laid out and used every maintenance day. In addition, have your junior NCOs teach maintenance classes. This ensures that they are competent, and it also ensures that your soldiers know what they are doing. You'll be amazed at how much your young leaders don't know about maintaining their equipment. Incorporating training into maintenance days is one way to significantly improve the quality of your unit maintenance program.

Refit and Recovery

In addition to quality command maintenance, you need to have a detailed recovery-from-the-field SOP that everyone understands and executes. The XO should lay these requirements out by day in a matrix on butcher block that is in a visible location during every recovery operation. The butcher block should have blocks next to every requirement for PLs/PSGs and

---

[60] For more information on change-of-command inventories, go to www.CompanyCommand.com and type the keyword "inventory" into the search engine.

commodity chiefs to initial as the tasks are completed. This allows for easy spot-checking by task and a quick assessment on how your unit is progressing through the recovery. We have posted our own light infantry refit and recovery SOP to the "Command Tools" section of www.CompanyCommand.com along with several examples from other branches and types of units. Every unit has unique recovery requirements. The point is that you need to have a detailed SOP for your unit that is strictly and routinely enforced.

Section 3. Safety

Ultimately, leaders will make decisions that place our soldiers in harm's way. That is inherent in the responsibility of command. We have tools to help you, and I expect you to use them but they are tools at best, and no tool can substitute for the exercise of responsible judgment. I expect commanders to create an environment in which the lives and well being of our soldiers are an integral part of the accomplishment of the mission.
– General Dennis J. Reimer, former CSA

Risk Management[61]

Risk management is a way of thinking that applies to everything you do as a military leader. Your challenge is to teach the process to your leaders and move the company to a mindset whereby they naturally make decisions using the risk-management process. Do not assume your leaders understand the process; take time out semi-annually to talk through it with team leaders and above using past and upcoming, inherently dangerous training as case studies. Then, reinforce risk management every time you train, and integrate it into your after action review process.

---

[61] *FM 100-14 Risk Management*, April 1998, lays out current doctrine on the risk-management process and is a reference every company-level leader should be familiar with.

Risk management is really a common-sense process that begins by simply identifying and assessing the possible ways that someone could get injured during a training event or mission given the task, conditions, and standards for the event. The next step is to decide how to mitigate the risk and control the possibility of those injuries happening. If you believe the benefits outweigh the risks, then execute the training with appropriate controls in place.

This thought process plays out in all training and tactical decisions. For example: Does the platoon leader decide to take a dirt road or to move across a very deep ravine (gulch in Hawaii) during limited visibility on their route to the objective? Soldiers could be injured moving across the ravine, it could take too much time, and the platoon might make too much noise. Taking the road on the other hand puts the platoon at risk to enemy ambush. Based on the situation, the platoon leader may decide that the benefits of taking the road outweigh the risks. If so, he needs to take action to mitigate the risks to an acceptable level. In this case he might develop a course of action that includes putting out an advanced guard, clearing high ground and other apparent ambush areas before moving through, etc.

What we are showing in this example is that the risk-management process must be applied in combat just as it is applied in training. From a strictly soldier safety-in-training perspective, one would consider the ravine at night to be the dangerous training for which the leader would mitigate risks prior to executing. In combat, it may very well be the road that is the more dangerous course of action due to the enemy situation. Risk management is a decision-making framework that is just as applicable in training as in combat.

Team leaders and above should carry an acetate-protected copy of your division risk-management worksheet and work through it every time they go to the field—not as a check-the-block exercise, but as a necessary part of caring for their soldiers. Forcing leaders to use the formal process will help them internalize and be able to use the process down the road as a matter of habit.

The most critical part of the risk-management process comes during execution, as risk management must be continuous to be effective. How many times have you discovered that conditions are different than expected once you actually get "feet on the ground"? Moreover, how many times have you witnessed conditions change during the actual execution of the training? Most injuries and accidents occur when leaders fail to recognize and respond to changing conditions. Typical conditions that change during execution include weather, light, terrain, and the physical and mental condition of soldiers. The mark of a good leader here is the ability to keep seeing the big picture and not to be blind to changing conditions once the unit is in the "execute mode." This ability usually only comes with experience. With experience, you will gain a sense of intuition or "gut instinct" that we encourage you to listen to. Make it a matter of SOP to take a break with your key leaders to review your risk assessment during the execution of dangerous training, especially when conditions change or something doesn't "feel right." In addition, ensure key leaders, especially you and the 1SG, are located where they can best assess and influence events as necessary.

Help your leaders to learn from their experiences by using the AAR process, especially whenever there is an injury or accident. We must openly discuss and learn from our failures as well as our successes! We have found in studying accidents that there was often one soldier who knew something was wrong before the accident occurred. Use the AAR process to bring this out for the entire group so that every soldier clearly understands they have an obligation to step forward if they know something is wrong. When every soldier begins to think risk management and understands their personal responsibility for it, you will witness a clear drop in injuries.

The Safety Briefing

Your weekly safety brief needs to be a huddle around you where you dialogue with your soldiers about life, personal responsibility, and the promising futures that they and their loved ones have. A reoccurring theme at your briefings should be personal responsibility and doing the right thing. You can help your soldiers see how one action can change the course of their lives. By making the safety briefing an important event, you can really have an impact on your soldiers over the course of your command.

Explain how important relationships are. Talk to them about their friends—constantly reinforce that the friends they keep will determine the direction of their lives. Talk to them about marriage and the commitment it takes—encourage them not to rush into marriage, as the person they marry will change their life for better or worse.

If you aren't charismatic or comfortable up front, get out of your comfort zone and do it anyway. Your soldiers don't expect you to give them a Patton speech, but they do need to see you and hear what's on your mind. Also, remember the amount of time you spent preparing for speeches you gave in college speech class? And yet, we often go out in front of the company without much thought—so work hard at what you will say to ensure that your soldiers leave with the message you want them to hear. It's what they hear that's important, not what you say!

Keep your briefings fun and don't worry about hitting all areas every time. One great way to do this is to use current stories from the paper. Another way is to have soldiers or junior NCOs join you in giving part of the safety brief. You can have the company vote on whether or not the brief was a "go" and then ask the company if the briefer missed anything.

Do not use a 3x5 card to brief safety. Imagine your dad when you were a senior in high school trying to read a list of do's and don'ts for the weekend—a complete turn off. If you simply read down a card, you will lose half of your audience from the start.

You must send a message to your soldiers that says you genuinely care about them and their future. Safety briefings are one great opportunity to regularly do so. However, make sure this isn't the only time you talk to your soldiers about life and safety. Constantly talk to them.

Safety and risk management should be integrated into everything that we do. Disciplined units and soldiers do not take unnecessary risks—whether in combat, training, garrison, or even off duty. Society has commissioned us to accomplish the mission, and our mission is inherently dangerous. However, when we do decide to place our soldiers' lives at risk, it is our duty to thoroughly analyze and mitigate the risks. In addition to safely conducting difficult training, leaders with a strong focus on safety engender tremendous trust from their subordinates, and they grow future leaders who will do the same.

Chapter Summary

A disciplined company is willing to pay the price to get ready for combat. Disciplined leaders understand that their sacred duty is to prepare their soldiers for combat, and they are willing to sacrifice in order to do so. This preparation begins with prioritizing and planning, steps that often are not given enough emphasis. The ideas we discussed in this chapter will absolutely help you better prioritize and plan your training, focus your maintenance, and be safer in the process. The things that we wrote about in this chapter will not *just happen*; take the guidon with a plan and start sharing your ideas and the workload (delegate) right from the beginning. Take one bite out of the elephant at a time, and you will be amazed at the incredible progress that you and your team will make.

Your Disciplined Company

- Make your company METL review process a team effort with all your leaders involved. Link the METL to critical collective and individual tasks.
- Within the first month, conduct an OPD/NCOPD on your unit's training-management process.
- Take time out every quarter with your leadership to plan the next quarter's training. The leader azimuth check/off-site will revolutionize the sense of team and collective vision in your company as well as bring sharper focus to your company's training management system.
- Use the "Rolling T" to manage your training management cycle.
- As a rule of thumb, when you evaluate training two levels down (squads), train one level down (platoons) concurrently.
- Use the training ideas and tips included in this chapter and via www.CompanyCommand.com to propel your training to another level.
- Use your change-of-command inventory as an opportunity to identify any areas in the company that need improvement and then begin improving them ASAP.
- Incorporate maintenance training on equipment into every maintenance day.
- Make safety and risk management an integral part of your outfit.

CHAPTER 3 -- PHYSICALLY FIT

Winning combat units are leader-driven, disciplined, fit, and motivated. Combat is without question the most physically and mentally exhausting thing one could do. In the wheel diagram that we used to describe a winning combat team, physical fitness was one of the three spokes. Although this chapter is not as long as the other three, we think physical fitness is of utmost importance, and it impacts everything else that your unit does. For soldiers to make effective decisions under stress and to have the stamina to accomplish the extraordinary things that they must, they have to be exceptionally fit.

Consider physical training (PT) to be the most important reoccurring training event that your unit does during the garrison duty day. Then, give it the emphasis that it requires. In this chapter, we will give you some PT ideas, focusing on assessing and planning PT.

Section 1. Initial Assessment and Company SOP

As you assume command and assess your company, you will want to evaluate the physical fitness levels of your soldiers. Do so in the context of your unit's combat mission. For example, the light infantry company mission would lead the new company commander to be especially interested in assessing foot marching fitness. This focus causes you to get away from simply looking at APFT scores.

Moreover, as you make your initial assessment, take a look at what training events are on the calendar over the next six months. For example, if you have an APFT scheduled two months from now, you will probably take a hard look at current APFT fitness levels. On the other hand, if your light infantry company is deploying to the Joint Readiness Training Center (JRTC) in six weeks, you will primarily be concerned with current foot marching fitness.

Some ideas to help you make your initial assessment:

- The absolute best way to assess your unit's physical fitness is to participate in unit PT and observe your soldiers in action. Check the PT schedule and then fall out with a different squad, section, or platoon every morning for the first two weeks of your command. Observe to see if the PT matches up with the plan, and assess the soldiers on their level of physical fitness. You are keying in on leader effectiveness, morale and attitude, and overall fitness.[62]

- Check the company personnel status daily, keying in on who is not conducting PT and why. Take a quick walk around the company area during PT formation to get a feel for how important your unit considers PT.

- Within the first thirty days of your command, conduct a company run and foot march if possible.

- Solicit your soldiers' feedback about PT in the unit. During your initial meetings with your leaders and soldiers, ask them about the current PT program. If you use a written survey in your initial unit assessment, include a question about the unit PT program.

- Ask to see past APFT scores and any other fitness data that is available.

- Meet with the division physical therapist and have her brief you on your company's profile statistics. Ask for trends in the division and for general advice on PT. Your battalion medical platoon leader and platoon sergeant will also be able to give you some good feedback on profile statistics. This

---

[62] Here is an example of what right looks like when it comes to PT. The leader begins by briefing the soldiers on the task, condition, and standard for PT that day. After stretching, the soldiers conduct challenging PT that matches up with the PT plan posted in the platoon area. Finally, the leader concludes with stretching and an AAR on the PT session. Hooah!

research would be an excellent developmental project for one of your lieutenants.

After you conduct your initial assessment, you will then want to establish how your company does business in the physical fitness arena. Get your company leadership together and talk about PT. Create a common vision for where your company is going.[63] Your leaders will likely agree that they want to have a great PT program—who wouldn't? Now, get them to describe a great PT program. One technique is to brainstorm in the group with one person writing the comments on a dry-erase board. Continuing this process, hone down the list to what you and your leaders agree are the most important aspects of a great PT program. The end result is a statement that describes your vision for PT. In addition, you can include more quantifiable goals and guidelines that will drive how you plan PT in the future. Here is an example of what your end product might look like:

Example Company PT Policy

- **We are battle-focused, physical maniacs**. Our PT program is challenging, fun, and progressive. We develop soldiers who can execute their combat mission in the most grueling conditions.

- **Centralized Planning**:
    - Company Master Fitness Trainer and 1SG plan the general company program 6 weeks in advance
    - Platoons publish general concept calendars 5 weeks in advance
    - Platoons publish detailed Task, Condition, Standards 1 week in advance

---

[63] Your meeting might start off like this: "All right team, I'm writing our company PT policy memo, but I don't want it to be just something that *I* come up with. I want to write what we really are all about when it comes to PT. Let's spend the next hour or so brainstorming and create something that will serve to inspire and guide us as we build a fit company."

Physically Fit

Example Company PT Policy cont.

- **Decentralized Execution**:
    - Majority of PT conducted at the squad level
    - Leaders held accountable for execution of PT

- **Specific Goals**:
    - 4-mile run in 32 minutes
    - 12-mile foot march in 4 hours, carrying 35 lbs.
    - Company APFT average of 270

- **Planning guidelines**:
    - PT is conducted five days a week (100% participation every day)
    - One foot march weekly (one 12-miler quarterly, one 20-miler annually)
    - Alternate upper body and lower body muscle workouts
    - At least one ability-group run per week
    - Keep running under 12 miles weekly unless building for a specific event
    - Minimum of two "Battle-Focused" PT events per month, e.g., casualty evacuation, individual movement technique (IMT) relays, obstacle course
    - At least one company motivational/unique PT session per month, e.g., off-post run, urban orienteering, aerobics

Section 2. Planning PT

Once you have developed goals and guidelines for your PT program, the next step is to actually begin planning. We recommend that you appoint on orders one or two people to be the company fitness experts who take the lead in PT planning. You might have a platoon leader/platoon sergeant team who are master fitness qualified and love planning PT, or a 1SG that lives to plan great PT. Either way, this person (or persons) will plan out the general company PT program.

Based on our experience, we find that planning an entire month at a time is the best way to go. When you do this, you see patterns and understand how things are—or are not—building toward the company goals. Moreover, you set up the company for success in that all the leaders know what days they have available to plan and conduct PT. Remember that you can't expect your leaders to plan great PT in advance if they don't know what days are theirs to plan. Lack of planning results in the "daily dozen" being the norm and lots of frustrated soldiers who know that PT could be better.

As you take command, develop a planning system that works for your company. Here we will give you one technique that is based on centralized planning and decentralized execution—it worked great for us. As we mentioned, you may designate a centralized PT planner to do this. Take a blank calendar and, while looking at the training calendar, identify all the days that are available that month for PT. Next, write-in the PT events that are already planned. For example, write-in the battalion run and the quarterly 12-mile foot march. Then, using the planning guidelines that you and your leaders developed, begin to pencil-in a general plan for company-directed PT. Using the above checklist, you might identify a day for the company motivational PT session, and days for company ability-group runs.

Example PT Planning Calendar

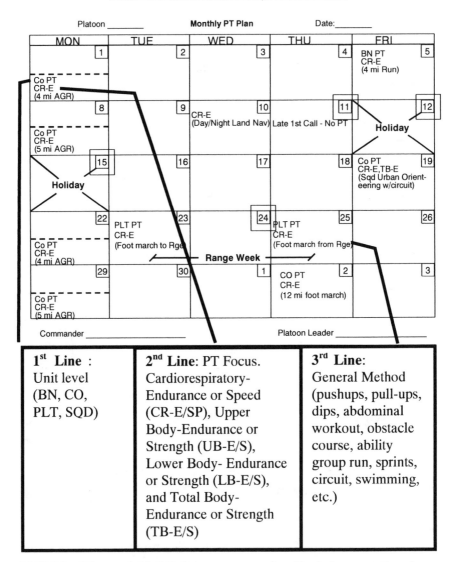

Platoon _____   **Monthly PT Plan**   Date:_____

MON	TUE	WED	THU	FRI
1 Co PT CR-E (4 mi AGR)	2	3	4	5 BN PT CR-E (4 mi Run)
8 Co PT CR-E (5 mi AGR)	9	10 CR-E (Day/Night Land Nav)	11 Late 1st Call - No PT	12 Holiday
15 Holiday	16	17	18	19 Co PT CR-E,TB-E (Sqd Urban Orient-eering w/circuit)
22 Co PT CR-E (4 mi AGR)	23 PLT PT CR-E (Foot march to Rge)	24 ← Range Week →	25 PLT PT CR-E (Foot march from Rge)	26
29 Co PT CR-E (5 mi AGR)	30	1 CO PT CR-E (12 mi foot march)	2	3

Commander _____   Platoon Leader _____

1st Line: Unit level (BN, CO, PLT, SQD)	2nd Line: PT Focus. Cardiorespiratory-Endurance or Speed (CR-E/SP), Upper Body-Endurance or Strength (UB-E/S), Lower Body- Endurance or Strength (LB-E/S), and Total Body- Endurance or Strength (TB-E/S)	3rd Line: General Method (pushups, pull-ups, dips, abdominal workout, obstacle course, ability group run, sprints, circuit, swimming, etc.)

NOTE: We used highlighter pens to visually bring out the days we were or *were not* doing PT. We used green for PT days and red for days when we were not conducting PT due to training or days off (e.g., holidays). Because this example is in black and white, we have placed an additional square around the days that would have been highlighted red so that you can clearly see what we are talking about.

In order to use this planning technique, you need to teach your soldiers how to use the system. You will want to include a list of abbreviations in your PT SOP to make sure all your soldiers can effectively read the calendar.

Lets look at some examples from the calendar above. On the 5th of the month, the unit is conducting battalion-level PT. The focus is cardiorespiratory endurance (CR-E). The method to achieve this endurance workout is a 4-mile run. The 23rd is an example of platoon PT. The focus is on cardiorespiratory endurance (CR-E). The method to achieve this endurance workout will be a foot march. The Mondays in this month are split to show that the first half of the PT period is open for platoon leaders to plan, while the second half is for company-level ability group runs.

After developing the company PT calendar, you or the centralized planner pass it out to the platoon leaders. We recommend that this distribution occur five to six weeks out so that you can provide visibility on the general plan in your training schedules. For example, during the last week of October, your platoon leaders should be completing the PT calendar for the month of December.

The platoon leaders, working with their subordinates, fill in the blanks on the monthly calendar, identifying the general plan for all the days that are available to them for PT. Having the company PT guidance as a checklist will focus their planning. For example, company guidance of foot marching one day a week, alternating upper body and lower body workouts, incorporating "battle-focused" events each month, and keeping running distances at 12 miles or less per week will help drive the platoon leaders as they build their PT plans.

Example PT Plan Filled Out By Platoon Leader

First Platoon   Monthly PT Plan   Date:_____

MON	TUE	WED	THU	FRI
Sqd PT 1 UB-E (PU, Pull-up, Dips) Co PT CR-E (4 mi AGR)	SQD PT 2 CR-S (IMT & Litter Sprints) LB-E (Abs)	SQD PT 3 CR-E (6 mi foot march)	PLT PT 4 TB-E (Aerobics) *Civilian Instructor	BN PT 5 CR-E (4 mi Run)
Sqd PT 8 UB-E (PU, Pull-up, Dips) Co PT CR-E (5 mi AGR)	SQD PT 9 CR-S (Sprints on track) LB-E (Abs)	CR-E 10 (Day/Night Land Nav)	SQD PT 11 TB-E (PU, Abs) *PM PT	Holiday 12
Holiday 15	PLT PT 16 CR-E (3 mi run) TB-E/S (Circuit)	SQD PT 17 CR-E (6 mi foot march)	PLT PT 18 CR-E (Swimming) *Pool is reserved	Co PT 19 CR-E, TB-E (Sqd Urban Orienteering w/circuit)
Sqd PT 22 TB-E (PU, Abs) Co PT CR-E (4 mi AGR)	PLT PT 23 CR-E (Foot march to Rge)	24	PLT PT 25 CR-E (Foot march from Rge)	SQD PT 26 CR-E (4 mi run) TB-E (PU, Abs)
		Range Week		
Sqd PT 29 UB-E (PU, Pull-up, Dips) Co PT CR-E (5 mi AGR)	SQD PT 30 CR-S (3 mi LMU run) LB-E (Abs)	PLT PT 1 TB-E (Div obstacle course) *OC is reserved	CO PT 2 CR-E (12 mi foot march)	PLT PT 3 CR-E (Swimming) *Pool is reserved

Commander _____   Platoon Leader _____

Green Highlight = PT Day	Red Highlight = No PT	Commander and platoon leader sign this as a contract

Using the calendar above as an example, the platoon leadership identified some issues based on the calendar they received from the company master fitness trainer. The red highlights helped to show that no PT was planned five days in a row (11th-15th) due to a long weekend and a late first call on the 11th. The platoon leadership therefore requested to conduct a pushup and abdominal workout at the end of the day on the 11th. In addition, they ensured that the first workout following the time off (the 16th) was a total body workout that included a run and a total body circuit.

Once the platoon leaders finish their tentative PT plans, you and/or the person you have designated to do so will want to check the plans. In addition to your company PT policy (See page 108), a checklist like the following one will be very helpful in ensuring that the platoon plans are in line with the company guidelines. We will go through this checklist using the previous platoon monthly PT example:

✓ **Long term focus and progression. What is the next major physical event? Is this month's plan building towards that event?** In this case, the next event is the 12-mile foot march. This platoon plan includes at least one foot march per week, except during the week that includes day and night land navigation. The company might have the soldiers carry alice packs during the land navigation to further prepare the soldiers for the upcoming 12-mile foot march.

✓ **Regularity and progression. Is there one foot march per week if possible?** See above.

✓ **Does the plan allow for recovery?** The example plan does a super job of alternating upper body and lower body muscle workouts so that the different muscles have time to recover.

✓ **Is there too much "red" on the calendar?** (Red highlight indicates days when you have no PT planned.) The first calendar had four "red" days and multiple days when no upper-body training was planned. The platoon leader noted this and made adjustments that resulted in a PT plan that was much more effective.

✓ **Is there at least one ability-group run every week?** Yes.

✓ **Does the plan keep running to 12 miles or less per week unless building for specific event?** Yes, this plan averages out to approximately 8 miles per week.

✓ **Are there at least two "Battle-Focused" PT events?** Yes, the plan includes individual movement technique (IMT) and CASEVAC sprints, foot marching, land navigation, and the division obstacle course.

✓ **Variety, balance, and motivation.** **Is there at least one motivational/unique PT session?** Yes, the squad urban orienteering, aerobics with a civilian instructor, the obstacle course, and swimming are all examples of motivational PT that add balance and variety.[64]

Finally, we had our platoons turn in a detailed PT plan for their platoon one week in advance. For example, on Monday the 22nd, the platoon leader would turn in a detailed plan for the week of the 29th. This plan would include the tasks, conditions, and standards for each day, and would specify by name a primary and alternate trainer for each PT session. The general calendar and the specific plan for the upcoming week were posted in the platoon areas so that every soldier knew generally what was coming up the next month and exactly what they were doing for the next two weeks. We believe this is a very reasonable and realistic expectation. Forcing your leaders to provide a detailed plan five to six weeks in advance almost always results in "checking the block" and plans that rarely are executed as briefed. On the company training schedule, we simply wrote Squad PT or Platoon PT and referred to platoon boards for specific tasks, conditions, and standards.

Although this exact system might not be for you, we highly recommend that you do plan a month at a time. It is the only way that you will see the big picture. By doing so you will see the occasional lapse in PT when you are in the field or perhaps off for a four-day weekend. If your leaders know that the benefits of your PT program decrease after 48 hours of not working a muscle, they will create innovative solutions that incorporate PT into the schedule. For example, they will begin planning PT in the field or in the afternoon when morning PT is not possible.

---

[64] Urban orienteering was a real team builder in our units. Each squad has a map and runs to points around post. The squad that gets the most points in the designated time wins. We were always amazed at how much harder soldiers ran when they were trying to win this competition. You can also include exercises at each point. Planning urban orienteering is a great special project for a junior NCO or an up-an-coming specialist.

Bottom line: The entire way you think about PT begins to change when you see it laid out on a monthly calendar.

Moreover, planning PT this way becomes a great way to develop your platoon leaders. Having them show you their completed calendar allows you to interact with them and help develop their planning skills. We remember making comments like these to our lieutenants:

- "We have a 20-mile foot march the first week of December and yet your platoon isn't doing a single foot march over six miles during the month of November."

- "I see that you are hitting lower body on Thursday, going into a four-day weekend, and then are planning on doing lower body again on Tuesday. That is six days without any upper-body work!"

Requiring them to lay out their PT plan a month at a time was the vehicle that led to this kind of leader development.

We also recommend that you don't try to get too specific in your PT SOP because every week is different. For example, if you say that you will foot march every Friday, you find that you might go weeks without a foot march due to long weekends, compensatory days, or when the training plan doesn't support it. It is better to say that you will foot march once a week and then schedule it given the context of the week. You may find yourself foot marching in from a training event that you otherwise would have ridden in from because you see it as the best opportunity to make sure you get the foot march in. Similarly, saying that Monday, Wednesday, and Friday are upper body days while Tuesday and Thursday are lower body days can put you in the situation where you aren't doing upper body for six days (long weekends).

Section 3. PT Ideas and Tips [65]

- **Educate your soldiers on overall fitness.**

Invite the division nutritionist into your company to teach your soldiers about the impact their diet has on their overall fitness. In conjunction with this, lead the charge against tobacco, drugs, and excessive drinking—all are ways we hurt our overall fitness.

- **Bring in a PT expert to teach an NCOPD.**

In the 25th ID (L) there was an outstanding officer, Tracy Smith, who was the division physical therapist. We invited her into our companies three times between the two of us to talk about PT principles, planning, and injury prevention. Her talks served as a catalyst for discussion and really got the unit to look hard at some outdated ways of doing things.

- **Inspect running shoes regularly.**

Poor running shoes combined with overuse are a leading cause of injuries. Bring in a professional to explain the importance of good running shoes and to train your leaders on how to inspect their soldiers' shoes properly. A typical young soldier or officer will take years to figure out how important this is unless leaders take the time to teach him or her.

- **Don't overdo running.**

Running 13 miles per week or more is high mileage for the average soldier and is asking for injuries. Run 3 times a week for 20-30 minutes, giving the body a rest day between each running session. Typical PT plans often include running every day,

---

[65] Although we validated these tips with our own experience, many of these ideas come from advice that Tracy Smith, our division physical therapist, gave us.

which leads to overuse injuries. Moreover, do not increase your running mileage by more than 10% per week.

- **Incorporate ability-group runs.**

Ability-group runs are a fantastic way to improve cardiorespiratory fitness, especially in large units. Unit cadence runs, on the other hand, are a great way to build unit cohesion, and they do provide a gauge for the commander to assess the unit's level of fitness. However, they do not improve soldier fitness the way that ability-group runs do.

- **Always stretch properly.**

Spend about 10 minutes stretching both prior to and following a workout. Hold each stretch for 10-20 seconds and repeat three times. As you stretch, tell the soldiers what muscle you are stretching. This teaches soldiers and helps them focus on the correct muscle.

- **Battle-Focused PT.**

Train for the PT test 6-8 weeks out, but otherwise tailor your PT program to support your METL. One idea is to have one of your lieutenants work with your NCO master fitness trainer to develop a physical program that includes battle-focused events that build the endurance, strength, flexibility, and agility your soldiers need to be effective in their combat mission. Tied to this is the idea of incorporating PT into field exercises. Simply stated, if you don't do this, your PT program will never be progressive! Soldiers will grumble at first; however, once you communicate the vision and they see a coherent PT plan laid out a month at a time, they will take pride in being in a unit that is dedicated to physical excellence.

- **Monitor soldiers' loads on foot marches.**

Ensure you have a weight standard for each foot march, and actually weigh alice packs. Begin with 20% of body weight and progress to no more than 40% of body weight. Remember that you don't run marathons to prepare for marathons; likewise, you should not carry max loads on every foot march. You need to watch new soldiers and be flexible here. Once soldiers are "foot march fit," a 40-50 pound alice pack standard will keep them where they need to be; much more than this will provide diminishing returns with higher rates of injuries. Additionally, ensure your pace matches your load and distance.

- **Special PT.**

This is for soldiers who don't meet the Army standard for physical fitness and/or weight. Identify someone to plan and supervise special/remedial PT, or else it will never happen to standard. Have your remedial program focus on cardiorespiratory, low-impact workouts using machines like the treadmill and bike. Remember that overuse is not going to help them out in the long run, so focus on low-impact training. The abdominal muscles are typically weak in most out-of-shape young soldiers. Moreover, abdominal muscles have a direct impact on all other forms of exercise. Abs can be worked daily, so include developing them in any remedial PT program.

- **Profile PT.**

This is conducted during normal PT time and must be run at company level to be effective. Again, you have to place someone in charge of supervising/leading this one or it won't happen to standard. Send your appointed leader to the physical therapy clinic to discuss your unit profile PT plan and get some specific input on the profiles you currently have. If you do this, you will reap the rewards, which include helping young soldiers rehabilitate more quickly and safely. You will also show the unit that you are serious about PT, both profile and regular.

- **Reception and integration.**

Without clear guidance on how you want new soldiers integrated into your unit PT program, they will typically be expected to perform at your unit's current level as soon as they sign in to the company. This will inevitably lead to injuries and works against what you are trying to achieve. If your leaders understand your expectations in this area, they will take the initiative and allow new soldiers to work up to your unit's physical fitness level.

- **Incentives.**

Your unit's PT incentives say a lot about what you think is important and can serve to focus and energize your soldiers. If you say that you value battle-focused PT, but only reward soldiers for their APFT performance, you are not being consistent. Moreover, if you say that you value teamwork, but only reward individual performance, you again are not matching rewards with your espoused goals. Here are a few ideas to spark your thinking:

PT Incentive Ideas	
Events/Standards	**Reward Ideas**
APFT – Squad with 100% scoring 270 or above **APFT – "300 Club" for individuals** **Orienteering – Best Squad** (Could be urban or field orienteering)	• Squad PT Trophy • Squad 3-day pass • Plaque with individual dog tags • Individual 3-day passes • Unit Coins • Silva Compass
Squad Battle-Focused PT Test – Foot March, Rope Climb, Buddy Carry, Pull-ups, Dips	• Certificates of Achievement • Squad Champion Belt

Your Physically-Fit Company

- Conduct an initial physical-fitness assessment of your unit in the context of your company METL.
- Develop a company PT SOP that will guide all your PT planning and execution.
- Plan PT a month at a time.
- Educate your leaders. Build a core of leaders who are experts at planning and executing physical training.
- Make PT planning centralized, but PT execution as decentralized as possible.
- Ensure the company progressively prepares for demanding PT events.
- Include PT in your unit field training.

CHAPTER 4 -- MOTIVATED

It is not enough to fight. It is the spirit which we bring to the fight that decides the issue. It is morale that wins the victory. – General of the Army George C. Marshall, 1948

Exceptional leaders build winning teams of disciplined, fit, and motivated warriors. The third and final spoke of our framework—the motivated spoke—completes the wheel and also this book. It is not enough to be disciplined and fit; like General Marshall stated, morale is indispensable to winning in combat. As you prepare for and command your unit, you will want to develop a well thought-out program to build the morale of your unit. This stuff doesn't just happen, so read this chapter and let it spark ideas that will work in your own situation.

We will primarily focus our attention on ways to positively impact morale by establishing a great command climate and by taking care of the soldiers entrusted to your care.

However, before we get into our recommendations we would first like to emphasize that "mission accomplishment builds morale and esprit far more often than the other way around." [66] Think about it. No soldier wants to be on a losing team, especially when losing in combat means death! As you seek to balance mission and soldiers, consider that the best way to take care of soldiers and build morale is to properly prepare your unit for combat. It is your sacred duty. Put another way, if soldiers aren't confident in themselves, their fellow soldiers, and their leaders, then no amount of pizza parties and time off will matter.

---

[66] Dandridge Malone, in *Small Unit Leadership,* 1983: p. 80. He goes on to write, "When soldiers and units get done those things that soldiers and units are supposed to do, that's when morale and esprit get highest ... That's why unit esprit is at its peak when the unit has a good FTX going out in the field ... As you build leaders, this law—Mission Must Come First—has to be, flat-out the cornerstone of your foundation."

Section 1. Command Climate

A key component of soldier motivation has to do with the unit environment. This is common-sense stuff:

Great Command Climate = Higher Morale = Better Performance

What exactly is command climate? FM 22-100 defines an organization's climate as the way its members feel about the organization and goes on to say:

Climate comes from people's shared perceptions and attitudes, what they believe about the day-to-day functioning of their outfit. These things have a great impact on their motivation and the trust they feel for their team and their leaders.[67]

There are obviously many things that impact the unit's climate. In this section, we will share our thoughts on three topics that we believe are especially important to creating a great command climate: trust, communication, and your reception and integration program.

TRUST – The Essential Ingredient

In many ways, the climate of your unit will be driven by effective relationships. At the root of all successful relationships is trust. Every single article and book that we have read about leadership and building winning teams has mentioned the importance of trust. Whether it is General Reimer (former Army Chief of Staff), Coach K (Duke basketball), Peter Drucker (management guru), or any of a hundred leadership authors and successful combat leaders, they all speak of the power and influence that trust has on teams. It is the often-mysterious factor that makes winning teams so great. We will give you our

---

[67] Department of the Army, *FM 22-100 Army Leadership*, 1999: p. 3-12.

thoughts on trust, but we acknowledge that they do not begin to illuminate the importance and complexity of the subject.

Do you love soldiers? Do you love *your* soldiers? Maybe we should stop here, because if your answer is truly yes, it will seep through your pores in ways that we cannot adequately describe. If your answer is unsure, this too will be evident to your soldiers, no matter what great techniques you wield to convince them and yourself that you care.

So, at the root of building a motivated team and establishing trust is how you fundamentally view the humanity that is your soldiers. Do you value and respect your soldiers and consider them equals? Do you believe that all soldiers are special in and of themselves regardless of race, religion, gender, or even performance? Treating others the way that you would want to be treated is the rule that should guide every leader's behavior. Your influence as a commander depends on whether or not soldiers believe that their concerns and needs are as important to you as your own. Having this kind of genuine respect for soldiers will set the conditions for trust.

Another critical issue affecting trust is integrity—both yours and that of the other element in the relationship. Words whisper and example thunders, or as one old CSM once said, "The longer I live, the less I pay attention to what people say and the more I pay attention to what people do."[68] So make sure your actions match up with your words. And true integrity goes beyond being consistent in word and deed. The Greek philosopher Heraclitis said, "The soul is dyed the color of its thoughts." Consider this: real integrity is being consistent in *thought*, word, and deed. In other words, it is not enough to do what you say. You must actually believe what you say and do if you expect to be taken as genuine.

Trustworthiness is the foundation of trust. If you want to be trusted, you must be trustworthy. The bucket of trust is filled one eyedropper at a time. Stephen Covey describes it as a bank

---

[68] CSM Cobb as quoted by John J. Maher when he was the Assistant Infantry Commandant at Ft. Benning in fall, 1994.

account that is best built by regular deposits over time.[69]   With this in mind, ask yourself whether your behavior is making deposits or withdrawals in your subordinates' trust bank accounts. If you truly have the best interest of your soldiers at heart in all that you do, you will be successful.

You must always do the *right thing* as a leader. If your soldiers observe you doing the wrong things, even when they are not directly affected, they will not be able to trust you. Consider the company commander who puts down one of his platoon leaders in front of another platoon leader. That platoon leader will wonder if the CO talks about him in front of others when *he* makes a mistake. Putting down the battalion commander in front of your subordinates is equally damaging, and in addition to sapping trust, in effect gives your subordinates permission to put you down in front of their subordinates. Every time you do the wrong thing, you build a hidden wall between you and your subordinates, while doing the opposite removes the walls. Over time, a commitment to doing the right thing will begin influencing the decision making of all your leaders.

We observed a situation that is worth relating here. At the conclusion of a training exercise in which Tony's company was the OPFOR for a National Guard battalion, one of his platoons discovered a cache of radio batteries. The platoon leadership planned on keeping the supplies. Before Tony could do anything, his 1SG stepped in and said, "NO—we will return the batteries and there is no discussion necessary!" The 1SG created so much trust with that one action. Not only did it establish what was expected in the unit, but it also caused everyone, including Tony, to trust him more. The 1SG's actions reinforced the fact that he would do the right thing. This is an important phenomenon to be aware of. Whenever a leader takes a stand for the harder right, he actually builds trust with soldiers in ways that seem totally unrelated to that particular event.

We also think of one of our brigade commanders, Gary D. Speer.   When we served on his staff, we trusted him because he

---

[69] Stephen R. Covey, A Roger Merrill, and Rebecca R. Merrill, *First Things First*, 1994.

made his intent clear up front and he was always dedicated to doing the right thing for soldiers. This gave us great freedom to make decisions at our level without feeling like we needed to get his blessing all the time. After working for him for a few months and understanding his thinking, we often didn't need to get his input; instead, we could simply ask ourselves, "What is the right thing to do in this situation?" We could speak with authority because we knew he would support us in doing what was right.

To return full circle to the introduction of this chapter, in combat, soldiers trust leaders who demonstrate competence. This is common sense—we trust winners, especially when the ultimate sacrifice is at stake. In addition, soldiers trust leaders who remain calm and think clearly under stress. If you are freaking out during training, your men are thinking, "If he is like this now, I don't want to be anywhere near him when the bullets are really flying." If you have been around a leader that remains calm in the worst of situations, you can appreciate how much trust is inspired by that behavior. If you struggle with remaining calm under stress, ask your RTO (or your 1SG or XO) to monitor this and give you feedback as necessary.

Trust is an essential ingredient of any winning team. It starts with who you are and it impacts every part of your organization. In closing, we recommend that you incorporate three things into your personal leadership philosophy, things that will promote a climate characterized by trust in your unit. They are:

- Do what you say you will do (DWYSYWD)[70]
- Do the right thing (DTRT)
- Don't sweat the small stuff (DSSS)

Being committed to these three things will help keep you focused and will make tremendous deposits into your soldiers' trust bank accounts. In addition, by daily emphasizing these concepts with your junior leaders, you are helping them develop a way of thinking that will impact the rest of their careers. You can see how your understanding of what you value and who you are—

---

[70] See Kouzes and Posner, *The Leadership Challenge,* 1995: p. 211.

knowing yourself—combined with a clear image of the future—vision—drive your effectiveness (See Vision, page 9).

Communication

Another element that influences trust and is an essential part of a great command climate is open, positive, and effective communication. Communication up, down, and sideways in the chain of command is an essential part of a successful team. In fact, much of effective leadership is really about effective communication. The first part of communication that often goes overlooked is listening. Listening to what is going on in the outfit is an art in and of itself. The first requirement is that you actually want to hear the truth. The next step is getting out there and doing it. Most important things take time, and listening certainly requires a lot of time. However, it is one sure-fire way to reinforce the trust we wrote about in the preceding section. Your soldiers will begin to believe that you care about them when you take the time to really listen and connect with them. When you communicate, you certainly want to use the chain of command; however, you will never be effective if you only listen through your platoon leaders.[71]

The second part of communication is effectively communicating information and intent to your company. It is easy to get caught in a self-defeating trap of keeping information from the people who need it the most. Information is power, and many Army leaders are trained to think they need to control

---

[71] A great story in Dandridge Malone's book, *Small Unit Leadership* (p.36) outlines this point. A platoon leader asked his battalion commander how it was that he knew so much about what was going on in the outfit to include things in his platoon that hadn't gone through the chain of command. The commander responded, "Look, that's a main part of what being a real commander requires. A commander may not always know best, but he damn well better always know most...Now and then, some guy will bitch about me 'violating the chain of command.' That's horse manure. I use the chain of command to command with. I'll communicate any damn way I can—up, down, sideways. I'll do whatever I can to make sure I know what's going on in this outfit."

power. The truth is that the more you try to control, the less you will be able to control. Get the information out there! Communicate expectations, what the unit's priorities are, and how you think the unit is doing. Encourage dialogue and idea sharing. Once your subordinates believe that they can influence the future, they will be committed to it. Open communication will allow this to happen.

Communication Ideas and Tips

• **Use Backbriefs**.

Backbriefs are critical to effective communication in both tactical and garrison situations. We know that backbiefs are critical during tactical planning and operations, and become increasingly important as leaders get worn down. In addition, backbriefs will make a tremendous difference as you communicate with your leaders while in garrison. Take the time to have your leaders tell you what you told them. Here is one way to do it: "To make sure that I communicated effectively, could you share your understanding of what I told you?" You will be amazed at how this technique will improve communication between you and your leaders. You will also see how many previous misunderstandings and frustration over confused expectations could have been avoided.

• **Write to Soldiers and Families.**

Publish a quarterly newsletter. Tell the company what they have accomplished, recognize achievements, welcome newcomers, and say goodbye to soldiers and families who are departing. Send out a weekly commander's note. Even one paragraph per week will have a big impact over the course of your command. Post it in the barracks and send it out on your e-mail distro to soldiers and families. One technique is to include two sentences on last week, two on the priorities for the upcoming week and a quote or joke to keep things interesting.

- **Establish a Company Web site.**

Now that just about everyone—including single soldiers in the barracks—is "on-line," we highly recommend recruiting a team of young soldiers to build and run a company Web site that facilitates communication and team building. The ideas are limitless. Use the Web as a communication multiplier; however, do not do so at the expense of face-to-face leadership, which is much more important.

- **Walk around (Leadership by walking around).**

Regularly schedule time to simply walk around your unit area to observe and get to know your soldiers. A few minutes regularly done is all you need here. This works in the field as well as in garrison. Do a little informal polling to see if your soldiers know what is going on.

- **Talk with soldiers on duty.**

Make a point to spend ten minutes talking with your CQ daily. Ask them about their families, their background, their aspirations, and hobbies/interests. Moreover, develop a written survey with a couple questions for each CQ to fill out. The questions should relate directly to unit priorities/goals—the feedback will be one more gauge for you as you continually assess current reality in your unit. Finally, have some sort of professional reading at the CQ desk that you require the CQ to read and summarize in one written paragraph for you.

- **Meet once a month with squad leaders.**

Have lunch or meet under a tree with your squad leaders on a regular basis. Start off each meeting with a recap of the critical issues that came up during the last meeting, and get feedback on where the unit is at on these issues. Listen to what is on their minds. You will usually discover an issue that is frustrating them but is based on a misunderstanding or poor communication. Use the opportunity to clarify. This is the absolute best technique to find out what is really going on at the level of leadership that will make the difference for your unit. However, it takes thick skin and a real commitment on your part. Remember that a good squad leader will be motivated just knowing that you will take the time to regularly seek their input.

- **Have a Leader Breakfast Program.**

Regularly eat breakfast with your leaders in the mess hall or at a local restaurant. Another great idea is to have platoon leaders over to your house for breakfast every other month. You can have platoon sergeants over on alternate months. The time will serve as an informal opportunity to bond and communicate. You might combine this with leader PT and even short OPDs.

- **Take PCS/ETSing soldiers out to lunch as they depart the company.**

Bring a notebook and ask specific questions like, "What is one thing you would change if you were the commander?" or "How could we be better trained?" Use your company goals as a springboard for questions to gain insight into how well the unit is doing. You will find out more than you could ever imagine about what is going on in the company, especially from ETSing specialists who have no reason to blow smoke. This is not a witch hunt; it's just one more way for you to get the full picture of your own unit.

- **Make use of every award presentation, reenlistment, and promotion ceremony and safety brief.** They are great opportunities for two-way communication.

Much of the art of leadership is wrapped up in communication—**you may be the most brilliant thinker, but if you don't listen to soldiers and communicate your ideas, heart, and intent effectively, you will not lead effectively.** We know that lack of effective communication is at the root of most leadership problems. Poor communication leads to frustration and eventually to poor morale. Each of the communication ideas listed above takes time. However, when you consider the benefits, you will get excited and block out time on the calendar for those activities. Don't let the urgent things keep you from something so important.

On a final note, remember that you are talking to soldiers; what they hear matters much more than what you say. If you want to capture their hearts and minds, you must learn to relate to them. The audience for which you write things like policy letters, your command philosophy, etc. is the soldiers of your company, not your platoon leaders or the battalion staff; constantly learn how to communicate and relate better to your soldiers. Use your RTOs and 1SG as sounding boards to help you with this.

Reception and Integration

The reception and integration of new soldiers is one of the most important programs in your company. We include it in this section because it is critical that you influence the way that incoming soldiers think about the organization and their role in it from the very beginning. You continue to shape the climate of your unit with the integration of every new member.

Whether or not you have a plan, reception and integration is happening and the process is typically complete after 10-15 days. Consider the first ten days as a window of opportunity that will close quickly. By the end of that period, most soldiers' long-term patterns have been set in motion. The people they are hanging out with and the expectations they establish for themselves in these early days will influence the rest of their time in the unit. Ensure that you use this critical time period to mold a future warrior and leader; don't leave it to chance. We recommend having your 1SG or a senior NCO lead this critical program.

What can you do and what can you get others to do to use this "first ten days" concept to your advantage? Well, first we will talk about what *you* can do. It starts with you meeting with the soldier—ensure you sit down with every new soldier and leader who comes into your unit (treat every soldier as a future leader). This meeting is part of forging the future for not only this soldier but also for the unit. Your mission is to communicate to this new member the unit vision and the fact that he or she is a critical part of that important vision. Provide each soldier a hard copy of the unit vision and goals and ask him or her to be a part of achieving it. We recommend that you write a letter home to the soldier's parents, which is all part of showing that you really care about each individual (See the "Cmd Tools" section of CompanyCommand.com for several great examples of letters home to parents). Soldiers must walk out of the meeting excited about the fact that they are expected to be a key part of something significant and also that the company leadership really cares about them.

Using a checklist like the one below helped us remember all the things we wanted to communicate to our new soldiers. It also ensured that we took time to listen to them. Finally, having information such as family members' names, a local address, and even the soldiers' thoughts on long-term goals proved to be invaluable to us during our time in command.

Example Commander's Interview Checklist

- Welcome, I really value you/You are important to the winning team!

- Name/Rank _____

- Squad/Platoon _____

- MOS/Job _____

- Family? Names_____

- Local Address _____
  _____

- Problems? (Pay, Housing, etc.)

- Previous experiences? Hobbies?

> This is where you discover your unit artist, photographer, computer genius, etc.

- Fill out re-enlistment card (Include near-term and long-term goals)

> Keep a stack of blank cards in your desk – after the meeting, pass the card on to your re-enlistment NCO. This will save you a lot of time in the long run.

- Discuss unit vision and goals and upcoming training highlights

- Provide the soldier a personal challenge to succeed from the commander

---

- Critical things you must do:
    - Drink responsibly (no underage drinking or DUIs)
    - Obey the law (do not use illegal drugs)
    - Treat soldiers, civilians, and your family with respect (no abuse or harassment tolerated)

- Letter home to mom and dad. Address

_____

_____

_____

Commander's Open Door Policy

Most soldiers really appreciated this letter, and moms and dads will write you letters of thanks. If a soldier's parents are divorced, you can send a letter to both. When in doubt, ask your soldier.

Another great reception-and-integration idea is to introduce new soldiers to the company during your weekly safety briefing. Remember that you are building a team. It is sad to say, but if you don't take the time to do this, most of the company will barely be aware that you have new soldiers, let alone know their names. Make the introduction a positive and fun event. Ask new soldiers where they are from and take questions from the audience. What a great opportunity to make new soldiers feel welcome and to demonstrate to the company how important new people are to you and the team. End the introduction by reminding the company that the new soldiers are the future and are the ones who will carry on the company's traditions and vision.

A priceless activity that we did was to have married soldiers and their spouses over to our houses for dessert shortly after they in-processed. If you do this around once a quarter, you will have a tremendous impact on the reception and integration of families. Ensure key personnel like the Family Readiness Group (FRG) leader, the 1SG and spouse, and the new soldiers' chains of command are present if possible. The spouses will meet their soldier's chain of command and also other new spouses. The concept of FRG will not seem so intimidating to them once they have a face to a name, and if they never come to another event you have at least seen them once. This is really a low cost event (dessert and very little time) that will have tremendous long-term benefits for the company.

What can you get others to do during the all-important first ten days to have the desired impact on a new soldier? The most important thing you can do is enroll your leaders—every platoon sergeant and platoon leader must believe in the importance of reception and integration. Ensure each level of leadership has an action plan to focus on new soldiers up front, to include their first few weekends. Take care of new soldiers' problems, get them assimilated into the squad, and show them what the positive norms of the unit are. Finally, ensure that the 1SG places two young soldiers on special assignment to bring the new soldier on board.[72] We know that the real socialization will typically occur with soldiers of similar rank and age, so don't rely solely on a great plan by the chain of command. Putting new soldiers with peer role models will go a long way to getting them on board the right way.

Cohesion Side-Bar

Cohere: 1. To stick or hold together in a mass. 2. To be logically connected. To cause to form a united or orderly whole.

Cohesion: 1. The act, process, or condition of cohering. 2. The mutual attraction by which elements of a body are held together.

History has proven that cohesive combat teams stick together under extremely difficult circumstances and form a "united whole" that is able to accomplish extraordinary things.

---

[72] Dandridge Malone, *Small Unit Leadership*, 1983: p. 75.

We believe that winning teams, by definition, are cohesive. If you do the things we discuss in this book—build a winning combat team—the result will be an extremely cohesive team.

Having said that, it is important to note that there are circumstances when cohesion can be dysfunctional. As you take the guidon and conduct your initial unit assessment, you will want to be aware of it. We were introduced to this concept by Scott Snook—a former company commander, combat veteran, Harvard Ph.D. and USMA Leadership Professor—and take the following quotes and chart from *Leadership in Organizations*, 1988: p.142-143. "Recall that norms are informal rules of behavior established by the group. The greater the cohesiveness of a group, the more influence the group will have over the behavior of its members. Consequently, the norms in a highly cohesive group will have a greater influence on behavior than the norms of a group with low cohesiveness."

Using the chart below, imagine a highly cohesive unit with low performance norms. This would be the most difficult type of unit for a leader to try to change. In many ways one would be better off taking over a unit with low cohesion but performance norms that were functional and in-line with the Army's core values.

		Low	Hi
Cohesion	Hi	Low Performance	High Performance
	Low	Low Performance	Medium Performance
		Low	Hi

Performance Norms

Section 2. Taking Care Of Soldiers

Morale is the greatest single factor in successful war... In any long and bitter campaign morale will suffer unless all ranks thoroughly believe that their commanders are concerned first and always with the welfare of the troops who do the fighting.
– General of the Army Dwight D. Eisenhower, 1948

Awards & Recognition

An innovative and active awards-and-recognition program is one of the most powerful ways we know to build morale and to reinforce the unit's values. The commander must be personally involved for the program to be successful.[73] We believe strongly that words, ribbon, paper, or time off is of negligible cost when compared with the results that they often inspire. Why limit awards or only award soldiers who do incredible things? We have heard people who aren't big on awards say, "He was just doing his job." Well, *just* doing your job as an American soldier deserves more recognition than any of us could ever give. Seek out every opportunity you can to recognize and award soldiers. There are hundreds of ways to do so, from a simple pat on the back to a medal. Later in this section we will share several ideas that were effective for us.

Remember that small achievements often precede big achievements, so challenge your leaders to keep their eyes open and see the small victories that, if encouraged, will lead to big victories. Leaders who continually look to catch soldiers doing something good will find more and more soldiers doing good. This is a paradox we have watched play out on several occasions. On the other hand, leaders who continually look to catch soldiers

---

[73] You establish the overall philosophy and personally get involved in the ceremonies. However, identify someone to take ownership of and manage the system. Typically it is the XO; however, Nate found that his 1SG was more effective in this area since he had better visibility on personnel departing or changing jobs.

doing something wrong will find more and more soldiers doing wrong. This is partly due to what you train yourself and your subordinates to key in on. However, it also occurs because soldiers live up to the expectations that their leaders have of them.

Ensure that award submission is a routine part of your refit and recovery SOP, and that you constantly talk about it. Often, leaders are too overwhelmed to make the effort it takes to get their soldiers recognized and awarded. If you make it an integral part of who you are as a company, you will find that the number of soldiers receiving awards will skyrocket. So will morale!

Always personally reward your soldiers and do so in front of the company. Bring the company in tight around you and tell them the story behind each award. Although we can't adequately express the impact that this will have on the soldier being awarded and every soldier listening, we will share a few reasons we believe you should do so. First, it reinforces the individual soldier's commitment. The fact that you know the story behind the award becomes very meaningful to the soldier, and goes way beyond the rote reading of the citation. Moreover, we know that soldiers want to live up to their reputation, and when you reward them in public they have a high standard to live up to.[74] We have often seen this become an almost self-fulfilling prophecy for young soldiers who are rewarded and begin to think of themselves as great soldiers.

Furthermore, when you share the awardee's story, you are really showing every soldier in the company what right looks like in a very powerful and meaningful way. You are giving the company real-life, real-time role models. Remember in Chapter 1 when we talked about vision and core values? When you tell the stories behind awards, talk about how the soldier's actions lived out the company's values and contributed to the team. Since teamwork is a value that you will want to promote, use the opportunity to reinforce it whenever possible. Bring the entire squad up front even if it was just one of the individuals in the squad who excelled. Allow the entire chain of command to

---

[74] Dandridge Malone, *Small Unit Leadership*, 1983: p. 96.

come forward and help pin on the medal. Also, invite families to participate whenever possible. Finally, capture these celebrations on film and post the pictures in the company area.

Soldiers want to be recognized and rewarded for hard work. When they see that excellence is valued and regularly recognized, they will work harder to achieve excellence.

Awards & Recognition Ideas and Tips

- **Company certificate of achievement.**

Create a company certificate of achievement and use it to reinforce and recognize excellence. Not only will it give junior leaders another option for awards, but it will also build unit pride. Have a design contest and award the winner the very first company certificate. Tony remembers NCOs specifically requesting the coveted company certificate in lieu of an AAM just because they had not received one yet. Nate made sure every soldier left the unit with one. A couple dollars at Wal-Mart will buy a frame that makes the certificate more personal. Having a company certificate program will take some work, but it is well worth it. One delegation technique is to have your company RTO or training clerk run the program with support from your XO or 1SG.

- **Develop competitions and unique and fun in-house awards**.

There are countless ways you can create healthy competition and innovative awards. Make a PLT PT award out of a weightlifting belt (similar to the WWF) and then have a monthly competition between the PLTs for the belt. With the belt can come different incentives (3-day pass, 2 days of sports for PT the next month, etc.); and, of course, during any company or battalion run it must be worn by a soldier from the current champion platoon. Other competition ideas include highest APFT average, tug of war, pugil sticks or king of the ring with platoon representatives, march and shoot. squad orienteering runs, and weapons qualification top gun to name a few—the sky is the limit. If your company organizes competition and rewards, you will find that the sense of teamwork and cohesion in your unit will begin to rise immediately. Again, healthy competition and fun and innovative awards breed excellence.

- **Recognize squad performance.**

Following every field exercise, award the best squad a plaque or a company certificate. The squad could be selected based on pre-established criteria or subjectively chosen by you, the 1SG, and the XO. Besides the obvious benefits, this is also a good way to create opportunities for excellence on your squad leaders' NCOERs. Make sure the squad that actually performed the best is recognized every time rather than letting the award get rotated based on which squad has not received it yet. If you allow your subordinate leaders to simply rotate the award, cynicism will set in and it will become a joke rather than a coveted award.

- **Have a "Bent Bayonet/Toad/Soup award."**

It doesn't matter what you call it, but once a month pull the company in and have each platoon run a skit for nominations for the award. Especially after a field problem, you will find some of the best laughs come out of this. Again, if you do this you will see the sense of camaraderie in your unit increase immediately. Then present the award to be displayed in the winner's respective office or platoon CP. Of course, your soldiers will usually be gunning to give you the award, so have thick skin—and have fun with it. If you get defensive or insecure, you will do more harm than good. Being able to laugh at yourself sends a powerful message to the company and serves to bond the team together.

If you want to create a team of soldiers who are motivated about what they do, are committed to the team, and achieve excellent results, then you will want to have an innovative, active, and positive awards program. Moreover, you will want to develop leaders who actively seek out and reward excellence.

This program will provide a balance to tough standards and UCMJ; consider it an injection of positive adrenaline that will make motivation a reality. Encourage your soldiers at every turn. Tell them what great things they can achieve as a unit and individually, and recognize them when they do so.

Counseling and OER/NCOERs

An effective counseling program is essential to the personal and professional development of every soldier in the company. Taking the time to do this right gets at the very heart of taking care of soldiers. Moreover, the amount of attention you give your subordinates' reports (OERs/NCOERs) speaks volumes about your commitment to them. In Chapter 1 we discussed counseling as it relates to leader development. In fact, we believe the most important goal of counseling is developing the next generation of leaders, and the focus of feedback should be on learning and growing. If your subordinates feel like you are constantly assessing them, they won't be as open and will tend to be defensive when you give them feedback.

In this section we will briefly discuss some keys to counseling and NCOERs/OERs without regurgitating what most people already know. However, first we want to mention *FM 22-100 Army Leadership*, the Army Developmental Counseling Library, and the Army Developmental Handbook, all of which are great resources for counseling and development.[75]

Experts will tell you that role modeling is absolutely the most powerful way to affect people's attitudes and "who they are." In the Army's "Be, Know, Do" framework, you can see that who you are and what you know affects what you do. Much of the "Be" part, who you are, is influenced by the role modeling of important people in your life. If we were commanding again, we would be much more aware of our own role modeling, to include how we role modeled counseling and the OER/NCOER process.

---

[75] http://www.fm22-100.army.mil/ Army Leadership Homepage, http://www.counseling.army.mil/ US Army Developmental Counseling Library, http://www-cgsc.army.mil/cal/LRAD/JOLDH/default.htm *US Army Developmental Handbook.*

It is hard to fully appreciate the impact that your example has on your subordinates. Think about it: every day you are making history. Your attitudes, choices, words, and actions are being absorbed and repeated in ways that you will never be aware of. Your platoon leaders will especially be influenced by your example.

Your Officers

As you prepare to counsel your platoon leaders for the first time, think about the impact that your example will have on them. The way that they counsel their subordinates will be a reflection of the way that you counsel them. In addition to providing your officers a great example of how to counsel, talk with them about their plans for counseling their subordinates. In your teacher/coach/mentor role, why not take a few minutes to help the new lieutenant reflect on what he just experienced (initial counseling with the CO) and, furthermore, how he might best prepare for and counsel his own subordinates? So take the time to properly prepare for your counseling sessions. Here is an example agenda to use to prepare for and conduct initial counseling with incoming platoon leaders:

Lieutenant Initial Counseling Agenda

- Explain the purpose of the counseling.
- Ask him how he is doing -- "Tell me about your inprocessing. Where are you in the process of getting settled in? Do you have any issues I need to know about?"
- Discuss the unit vision and goals and review your OER support form with him.
- Review his duty description.
- *Briefly* identify his additional duties (the XO will go over in detail).
- Discuss your expectations of a new lieutenant (be able to provide this in hard copy via a counseling form). What should his "big rocks" be?
- Discuss the training calendar for the next quarter.
- Provide him a copy of all pertinent SOPs.

- Talk him through the new lieutenant certification process. ———— See page 46 for example.
- Provide him direct guidance for his 1st two weeks. Tell him to:
    - o Build a draft version of OER Support Form (tie it in to platoon goals)
    - o Conduct a self-study (current strengths and areas to improve, or "gaps")
    - o Draft his initial JODSF (Leader Development Action Plan). Direct him to include everything from the new LT certification program on the JODSF.
- Discuss OER rating chain.
- Talk about how he plans to counsel his subordinates.
- Allow him to ask questions and make sure he understands your guidance.

We recommend that, at the end of your initial meeting with a new lieutenant, you assign him a task that must be completed by the next day. His response and quality of work will give you a clearer picture of who he is—his attitude and concept of duty— and will give you a golden opportunity to clarify your standards and expectations. Nate had all newly assigned platoon leaders report to him prior to PT the day after he met them, with all their field equipment set up and marked according to the unit SOP. The purpose was two-fold. First, it ensured that the lieutenant went to his platoon setting the example in a simple but very visible and important area. Second, it gave Nate great insight into the lieutenant's character. When you do this sort of thing, make sure that you are very demanding in your inspection of whatever task you assign. If the lieutenant doesn't meet the standard, send him to the XO for guidance and have him report to you again the following morning for re-inspection.

One great technique to organize each of your subordinate officer's counseling packets is to use a three-section folder that has company goals on the left side, the lieutenant's OER Support Form and JODSF in the center, and monthly counseling forms on the right side. The company goals reflect the objectives on your

OER Support Form, just like the platoon's goals should reflect what is stated in the platoon leader's OER Support Form. The JODSF becomes the developmental action plan that we have been talking about (See Leader Development, page 50).

Company Goals Cdr's OER Spt Form	LT OER Spt Form Platoon Goals JODSF	Monthly Counseling Forms

Furthermore, your new platoon leader should create a counseling packet for his PSG that mirrors the packet you have on your 1SG but is tailored to his platoon. We recommend that you show the lieutenant your 1SG's counseling packet as the standard for what you expect of him.

Your NCOs

Many company commanders fall prey to not counseling their 1SG since, after all, the 1SG is senior and already knows all she needs to know. This is a grave mistake. We recommend that you set the standard for the company in your counseling of the 1SG. In addition to modeling what "right looks like" for the rest of the company, regular counseling will be one more way that you can develop open communication with the 1SG. The 1SG, just like any other soldier, needs feedback, and she needs to know that what she does is noticed and appreciated. If you don't provide feedback, who will? During each counseling session, discuss the company vision and goals, and how the company is or is not achieving those goals. Make this a collaborative exchange; the process will energize you both. Similarly, provide the 1SG some personal feedback and discuss a plan of action to better capitalize on her strengths and close her performance gaps. In addition, you can provide your 1SG with a written summary that captures all that the company has accomplished over the last month or two and summarizes what you discussed during the counseling session.

Here is one effective way to set up an NCO counseling packet:

Company Goals Biographical Sheet	Working NCOER NCOER Checklist	Monthly Counseling Forms

Work with your 1SG to project "excellence" and "success" bullets for the upcoming rating period, focusing in on the next quarter. You can write these in on an NCOER in pencil and then update them with what actually occurs (working NCOER), or you can create an NCOER contract that is nothing more than a counseling memorandum capturing what would constitute "excellence" and "success" bullets for the upcoming rating period. Either way, you are clarifying expectations and ensuring that you and your most senior NCO are working towards the same major goals and objectives. Writing the report at the end of the rating period will be extremely easy if you have been disciplined with counseling and updating the working NCOER.

In addition to counseling your officers and 1SG monthly (or after every major training event), we also recommend that you counsel your platoon sergeants and squad leaders following major training events. Here is an example of some questions that you can use as you counsel your subordinates with a focus on their development:

- What have you experienced or accomplished this period?
- What have you learned professionally and personally?
- Currently, what is your biggest leadership challenge?
- What is your focus during the upcoming quarter?
- How can you prepare yourself and your unit for the upcoming training?
- What are you doing to develop your subordinate leaders?

We again would like to emphasize how important it is that you give your subordinates' reports the same attention that you want given your own OER. Part of doing this is effectively communicating with the battalion commander about your subordinates' performances. Doing so will build incredible trust with your senior NCOs and lieutenants. Your investment here clearly demonstrates to them that you understand the contributions they are making to the team and that you care about their futures.

We have stated several times that trust is the key ingredient in effective relationships. One skill that most of us could work on and that builds trust is simply listening. Therefore, in your counseling, spend a lot of time listening to your subordinates, especially your 1SG. Before you tell her about all *your* wonderful ideas, take the time to listen to *her* ideas. Often, listening is preceded by a great question. One question that has proven to be extremely effective for both of us is: "What is one thing that I should know about you if we are going to work well together?" Much of the art of the question is in sticking with it. Repeat it and rephrase it in order to push the counselee to answer it honestly. **Bottom line:** Make developmental counseling, which culminates with the OER/NCOER, a personal priority in your unit. Set the example in your own counseling—especially ensure that you prepare for each session, and remember to listen sincerely.

Reenlistment Program

Your reenlistment program is a critical part of taking care of soldiers. The message of your program must be about each individual soldier's personal future and what is best for him. Although you want to retain good soldiers—the success of your unit and the Army depends on it—the soldier must come first. This kind of focus will engender trust from your soldiers and will result in more soldiers reenlisting in the long run, anyway. Put yourself in your soldiers' shoes and treat them the way you would want to be treated.

We challenged you in Chapter 1 to ask yourself why soldiers would want to be in your unit. If you build an exceptional unit—the kind of unit that soldiers want to be in—reenlistment will never be a stressful issue for you. After all, first-term soldiers' impression of the Army will reflect their impression of your unit.

Reenlistment begins with the initial meeting each soldier has with you (see reception-and-integration section earlier in this chapter), and continues until the soldier's reenlistment window closes. Have a stack of blank reenlistment cards in your drawer and fill one out during the initial interview with each new soldier. Hand the card off to your designated reenlistment NCO who will maintain the cards and track reenlistment for you.

Make sure you know who is in the reenlistment window. Your reenlistment NCO should keep you informed about this. Another technique is to have your platoon leaders brief their reenlistment status during command and staff meetings, thereby ensuring that they know when their soldiers are eligible to reenlist.

As soldiers come into the window, start talking to them about their options, both military and civilian. We found the best way to do this is informally, such as in the field or while eating meals. You and your chain of command want to get to know your soldiers' aspirations, goals, and desires. In many ways you will act as a parent who desires what is best for their child. You want your soldiers to be able to be all that they can be. Moreover, you want to make sure your soldiers are armed with correct information and are not misinformed. Ensure the message is very clear that you care about them, their future and what is best for them.

When a soldier reenlists, make it a celebration. Allow the soldier to choose the location for the reenlistment ceremony. Whenever possible, require the soldier's platoon to be there for it and encourage families to participate. Memorize the oath and have your platoon leaders do the same. This shows respect for both the soldier and the commitment that he is making. Personalize the reenlistment by telling a story about the soldier. Moreover, make sure there is a photograph plan and, following the ceremony, post pictures of the event in the company area.[76]

You can establish reenlistment incentives that communicate the value you place on reenlistment. (Each battalion will influence this, too.) One reward idea is to move a soldier who reenlists to the top of the schools list for the non NCOES-school of his choice. You can also make the reenlistment a celebration for the team by giving the entire squad of the reenlisting soldier a three-day pass. Be creative and find ways to show soldiers how much you appreciate their commitment to the Army.

When you and the other key leaders in the unit show genuine concern about each soldier's future, you send a powerful message about the value you place on your people. So use reenlistment as another opportunity to demonstrate genuine concern for soldiers and to reinforce the unit's values.

Promotions and Schools

These are two areas that are absolutely critical to the morale of your company. Units that cheat soldiers in these areas breed cynicism and undermine anything positive that the unit is trying to do. Soldiers want to be in a unit that does everything possible to promote and send deserving soldiers to schools. Your 1SG and NCOs will run these programs for you; however, it remains your responsibility to ensure that promotions and schools are indeed getting the attention they deserve.

---

[76] We recommend that you keep a photo of every reenlistment you do for yourself also. This will serve as a personal motivator in the future.

Part of your responsibility is to make sure your lieutenants understand enlisted promotions. A great idea is to assign one of your platoon leaders to give a presentation on enlisted promotions. He will research the subject, interview different NCOs—to include his PSG, the 1SG, and the battalion CSM—and then give his presentation to all the PLs, with the PSGs and 1SG in attendance to offer their feedback at the end. This is a great way to develop your lieutenants and to make sure the company leadership is on the same page when it comes to promotions. Another great learning technique is to send your LTs to a promotion board so that they understand and have a perspective of what their soldiers go through. Officers must understand how the enlisted promotion system works.

Schools are another key component of leader development and morale in your unit. Typically, your 1SG will manage schools in your company; however, you must be an integral part of the program. One way you do this is by celebrating success. Make a big deal out of every single graduation, and do something special for soldiers who demonstrate excellence in schools (e.g., Honor Graduates). Take time out to visit soldiers in schools. For example, go have lunch with soldiers who are attending PLDC. Take the 1SG and the attending soldier's PL, PSG, and SL along with you. Another way to show your support is to send a hand-written congratulatory note to each soldier who graduates from a school. In addition to learning valuable skills, your soldiers are representing the unit every time they attend a school. Tell them how much you appreciate them representing your unit so well.

Promotions and schools are critical to the morale of your soldiers. Put yourself in their shoes and do the things that would motivate and engender trust in you. Be the unit that aggressively seeks to promote and send deserving soldiers to schools.

Family Readiness Group

Think of the company as a family and the FRG as an extension of it. The primary reason that you have an FRG is so when you deploy there is an established network that allows communication to and from families and the unit. In addition, the FRG helps respond to family needs during deployments. When you are not deployed, you want to create opportunities to establish relationships, practice communicating, and respond to existing needs. We know that the more you do this, the more successful the FRG will be when there is a real deployment. Energy created here will help your organization move towards being a cohesive unit. The more creative you can be, the more successful you will be.

FRG Ideas and Tips

• **Company Parties.**

At least once a quarter have a company party where families are welcome. The key is to create activities where relationships are built and people have fun together. Keep expectations realistic. Make it fun for kids—at parties you can get a moonwalk, train ride, or costume (Santa, Easter Bunny, etc.) from the recreation center for a reasonable price.[77] As you plan parties, remember that you have soldiers of many different cultural and religious backgrounds. Recognizing and embracing the cultural diversity of your team will draw your unit together rather than create division. For example, celebrating Three Kings Day will broaden cultural awareness and will inspire your Hispanic soldiers to be proud of their heritage.

---

[77] We had company bowling nights every couple of months that included snacks, a quick spouses' meeting, and even hails and farewells. "Kiddie" lanes with gutter blocks helped make it fun for everyone.

- **FRG Meetings.**

Any FRG meetings you have should be run by the spouses—it is their group. Your role is to ensure the chain of concern is kept updated and to keep the spouses informed. One technique is to hand out training calendars for the upcoming quarter that boldly annotate field time, garrison time, and family events. This calendar is most effective when it is specifically tailored to spouses; the unit training schedule simply won't mean anything to most spouses. Whomever you have in charge of the calendar and updating the chain-of-concern roster needs to be proactive and "up to date."[78] An effective calendar combined with a good roster that shows people's names, phone numbers, and the names and ages of kids, will go a long way towards establishing your family readiness group. Develop innovative ways to communicate to your families. Create a company e-mail distro list and send out messages that way. Send notes through mail, personally call on the phone, make announcements at formation, post flyers, etc., but never assume that every spouse got the word.[79]

Do not get caught in the trap of having FRG meetings only in the company day room—most people naturally won't get very excited about hanging out in the day room with the same group of folks and crying babies. Tying your meetings into company parties is one innovative way to accomplish the mission.

- **Planning Key Events.**

Work with the FRG to decide what events they want to do over the upcoming year (e.g., holiday parties, single soldier dinners, deployment sendoffs, etc.), but do not try to do too much and do

---

[78] We chose to be personally involved with the chain-of-concern roster. It helped us stay abreast of all the new families in the company.

[79] If you personally call every spouse for your first event, you will have more turn out and you will begin to establish relationships that you never would have otherwise. A few calls a day and you can talk to every spouse in the outfit in one week.

not try to hit every holiday. Just make sure the events you choose are done with excellence. If it is something that will affect the entire company, then involve the chain of command and BOSS reps in the decision. Lay this on top of what battalion events are planned (battalion formal, etc) so you don't load too many events in one month. Also, don't lose sight of the focus—when your unit deploys, the FRG is a team that can support and care for each other. Your challenge is to figure out how to create a climate and opportunities that allow this to happen naturally, because you cannot force it to happen.

Better Opportunity for Single Soldiers (BOSS)

BOSS is another Army acronym that just boils down to taking care of soldiers and creating a cohesive outfit. This program should support the values and goals of the unit. We like it because it gets young soldiers involved in making a difference. Think about the pool of energy that is left untapped when you don't get your youngest soldiers involved. Your enthusiastic participation demonstrates that you care about them and it also enlists their efforts towards building a motivated team.

Ensure your monthly BOSS meetings focus on quality of life for the single soldier; don't turn them into sensing sessions for the company. One excellent meeting technique is for your company rep to meet with the platoon reps first to discuss issues, concerns, and ideas. Once that is accomplished, the BOSS reps can then brief you and the 1SG. You and your 1SG must take action on the concerns that your BOSS representative shares. If soldiers get no response, they will quickly become cynical. At each succeeding meeting, bring the notes from the last meeting and go over them, asking soldiers if each concern has been addressed yet.

Focus the energy of your single soldiers towards what they *can* do rather than on all the things they can't do. Help the BOSS reps to develop goals and general procedures for the way they will operate. One goal might be to schedule a bus at least once a quarter for the single soldiers to take a trip and see something.[80] Have your BOSS run tournaments out of your day room (pool, foosball, ping-pong, darts, etc). Don't try to do too much, but work to create opportunities for them to get out of the barracks and experience something together that they probably would not have done on their own.

Although this is a soldier program, you and your 1SG must be active participants and cheerleaders, especially in the beginning. Helping them to achieve a small win early on will build momentum that will lead to bigger wins. Challenge them to get involved and to do something to make a difference. Again, you are building the team. Once this program gets going, you will begin to see how it benefits the entire company.

UCMJ

UCMJ is an incredible tool that you can use to transform your unit; it can serve to reinforce the unit's values and goals, or it can severely undercut everything you are trying to accomplish. Look at every Article 15 as a critical event. Each one can be an NCOPD/OPD for the chain of command. The process establishes your principles, and it will either reinforce or undermine the trust that your soldiers—both the soldier being adjudicated and the chain of command that is participating—have in you. **Your goal is to affect change in the individual, the chain of command, and the entire company.**

One way to drastically erode trust is to skip members of the chain of command in this process. If you want team leaders to take responsibility for their teams, you can't afford to keep them out of the loop. Conduct UCMJ action on a soldier without the squad leader's intimate involvement and you have taken a momentous leap backwards in your efforts to build a winning team.

---

[80] Ideas in Hawaii include trips to Sacred Falls or the Arizona Memorial, snorkeling, laser tag etc. Be innovative. Nate's soldiers took trips to Kauai and the Big Island using National Guard Aircraft. Cost per soldier was $25 for the entire trip!

Make sure you seek out advice. Call your brigade legal advisor on all actions you handle until you have a breadth of experience to operate from, and if you have any question, call again. Your 1SG will probably be your greatest source of knowledge and advice on UCMJ. You will want to establish up front with your 1SG how you envision UCMJ working in the company. Also, do not be afraid to bounce issues off an experienced peer, the battalion CSM, or one of the battalion's field-grade officers.

You are making history every time you conduct an Article 15, whether you realize it or not, so give the process your full attention.

Running an Article 15

Ensure that you reinforce the chain of command every time you conduct an Article 15, beginning with having them all present for the hearing. Explain up front to the soldier and the chain of command what the charge and the possible punishment are. Give the soldier a chance to tell his or her story and to discuss matters of extenuation and mitigation. (Take the time to explain to each soldier what these terms mean.)[81] Do not assume you know exactly what happened. Really try to understand how the soldier was thinking. His perception of your understanding of what he is saying will open the soldier up for accepting what you have to say later.

One great technique is to have the soldier tell you what he did wrong and why his action was detrimental to the unit mission. They will surprise you with their honest answers. Ask the soldier what punishment he would impose on himself if he were the commander. This turns the table and makes the soldier see things

---

[81] Extenuating circumstances are circumstances surrounding the event that better explain why it happened. An example of extenuating circumstances for a soldier who was late to formation could be that his daughter had to be taken to the emergency room or perhaps the soldier was on 24-hour guard duty with only a one-hour rest. Mitigating circumstances have to do with the soldier's past record. In the above example, perhaps the soldier had never been late before and just won company soldier of the month.

in a new light. You can tell a lot about a soldier's attitude when you do this.

Have the soldier step out of the room and then discuss the soldier and event with the chain of command. Take punishment recommendations starting with the lowest ranking leader and always finish with the 1SG. You make the final decision. Call in the soldier and explain that you have listened to the chain of command and have decided on the following punishment.

Punishment must be focused on the soldier's future and it must match the soldier and the crime. Be consistently fair ... hard but fair. You will be respected for it. We rarely suspended punishment. If you do choose to suspend punishment, make sure that you tie suspension to a developmental plan, and that you establish a specific time period and criteria whereby you would invoke the punishment. Always tell soldiers the great thing about life is that you can do whatever you want; however, you must be willing to pay the consequences (which may impact you and others!). When they breach the code in some area, put yourself in the position of telling them to step up, take the consequence of their actions, and then move out in a direction that will ensure success—they are at a cross-roads. Ask them what they want to do with their lives and if their current actions are getting them there. Get them to think. They will understand and respect the dialogue.

Once you have imposed punishment, have the soldier leave and stand-by outside the 1SG's office. Take some time to review what happened with the chain of command. Use the time to teach, coach, and mentor the chain of command and to make sure they understand their role in the soldier's future development. Following the hearing, your 1SG should meet with the soldier and his NCO leadership to ensure the punishment is clearly understood.

The UCMJ process may have more impact on the climate in your unit than any other one thing you can point to. The good news is that you can determine whether it is a positive or negative impact. Create a climate where the chain of command knows that recommending an Article 15 is serious business. A rash of Article 15s may not reflect a lack of discipline as much as a lack of leadership and counseling. An Article 15 can at times be an easy leadership tool because it pushes the problem off to the commander. Discuss this area in depth with your 1SG when you assume command to ensure that there is consistency and that you both agree on how UCMJ will be administered in the company. Your goal is to effect change in individuals, leaders, and the entire company. Treat each Article 15 as a "decisive point" in the development of your company.

More Motivation Ideas and Tips

• **Single-Soldier Dinners.**

A great way to show your single soldiers how valuable they are is to have single-soldier dinners. You can either have the spouses provide homemade meals or work with the mess hall to ensure you have an especially good menu for the occasion. Tony once had his platoon leaders bring in ice-cream sundae fixings and act as waiters for the soldiers throughout the meal. Everyone loved this. Finally, invite someone like the CSM or the chaplain to say a few words to the soldiers. Again, this is a very low-resource way to build your team.

• **Unit History and Combat Veteran Program.**

Appoint a unit historian and discover your unit's history and lineage. The Internet is a great resource and way to link-in with veterans' groups. Read and post unit citations and awards earned by your outfit, and talk regularly about the courageous things that veterans of your outfit did. Tying your unit to the past will give your soldiers a sense of purpose and will inspire them to live up to their heritage.

In addition, link current training to the past. Nate's company named training events in honor of Congressional Medal of Honor winners. They read the CMH citation in a company huddle prior to training and talked about the values that the veteran displayed. A great technique is to have a soldier read the citation and lead the discussion. Soldiers want heroes—give them *real* heroes to be like!

Get retired NCOs and combat veterans to come in and talk to your soldiers. Imagine the effect on them when you bring in a former POW or combat veteran to talk about what the Code of Conduct meant in their personal experience. This one event will provide great energy for the unit; contrast that with the typical slide presentation by someone in your company.

The ideas are limitless, so tap into this incredible resource! There are countless combat veterans living near Army posts or still serving in units in your division—put one of your LTs in charge and start this one as soon as you take command. The veterans will consider it a privilege to share their experiences, and their service and example will inspire your soldiers.[82]

- **Photographs.**

Designate a company photographer and give him or her the mission of capturing shots of the company in action. Post the pictures and keep the board updated. For a few dollars at Wal-Mart, you can have instant 8x10s of your soldiers doing great things. Once the company office area is filled up, begin rotating pictures to the day room and the barracks. The possibilities are endless. Keep one area designated for pictures of award and promotion ceremonies. Capture soldiers on field problems, live fires, and off-post motivational trips. Whatever you choose to do, the end result will be a visual picture of the unit's past that

---

[82] As an example, 1SG(Ret) Acuna shared awesome insights from his experiences as a 25th ID LRRP with Tony's LRS detachment. Not only did 1SG Acuna inspire the soldiers, but he also became a visible connection to the history of the unit. When CSM(Ret) McGuirk spoke to Nate's company, he had an incredible impact on the men—so much that their training took on a renewed sense of passion. In fact, Nate's company named the next major training operation in honor of him—Operation McGuirk.

inspires commitment and simply gets soldiers excited about being in the unit.

- **Unit Motto, Art, and Memorabilia.**

A unit motto can have a powerful motivational effect on a unit. If your unit doesn't have one, take nominations and choose one. A motto that is tied into history and represents what you want to be about (Vision) will be a catalyst that will energize your outfit. Purchase art or encourage soldiers with artistic talent to paint murals around the company area. Finally, unit memorabilia will go a long way towards building unit pride and sense of uniqueness. Coins, hats, t-shirts, and coffee mugs are examples of the things that help build a sense of team. You want your soldiers to feel like they are part of something special. And remember you have plenty of talented and capable soldiers that just need a little encouragement—PFCs and specialists with talent and motivation can be your best workhorses in this area.

- **Soldier Dog-Tag Collection.** [83]

This awesome idea is specifically for *your* personal motivation. The only reason neither of us did this is because we found out about the idea too late. Collect a dog tag from every outgoing soldier in your outfit throughout your time in command, and hang them on a chain in your office. Prior to your change of command, collect a dog tag from the soldiers remaining in the company and take the chain with you. This chain will take on more meaning in the years following company command and will forever serve as a tangible memory of the soldiers who were part of your team. What a tremendous motivator!

---

[83] Tony Turpin shared this great idea with us while he was commanding in the 2nd Infantry Division in Korea.

Your Motivated Company

- Mission accomplishment drives morale.
- Integrity and competence are the critical factors that impact trust; all relationships are driven by trust.
- Words whisper, example thunders.
- The first ten days in a unit are your new soldiers' most important.
- Reward excellence and others will aspire to attain it.
- You are making unit history every time you conduct an Article 15 hearing.
- Start a leader breakfast program.
- Create innovative ways to include spouses, such as having new families over for dessert.
- Conduct off-site PT.
- Create a sense of history within your company.
- Communicate effectively and routinely. Your effectiveness as CO depends on your ability to communicate and connect with your soldiers— constantly plan how to best do this.
- Create a fun, team-spirited culture through creative awards and competition.

Conclusion – Where We Go From Here

In this book, we have described a framework for commanding at the company level, and we have shared many ideas and lessons learned from our own experiences. Our desire is that reading these pages has motivated and challenged you to become the best commander that *you* can be.

You will have your own unique command experience, and you will witness and develop different and effective ways of building a winning team. Although we certainly would love it if you applied what we have written, we would be even more excited if this book becomes a catalyst for you to begin sharing your own ideas.

We ask you to join in an Army-wide partnership of company-level leaders who are dedicated to creating winning teams. We see the Army not only as a collection of units but as a gathering of like-hearted comrades who are committed to living out a professional calling. Imagine the positive impact of thousands of Army leaders coming together to share leadership insights, ideas, lessons learned, and better ways of doing things. Your venue for this kind of lateral sharing of knowledge and experience are the CompanyCommand and PlatoonLeader professional forums (CompanyCommand.com and PlatoonLeader.org). Founded and run by a team of active-duty officers, these forums unleash the potential that exists when professionals join together to pursue excellence.

These are exciting times. The future is bright. Join with us and be a part of making a difference for our Army.

Read on to find out more about CompanyCommand and PlatoonLeader.

We would sure love to hear from you.
Your feedback is a gift that will directly impact our ability to serve company-level leaders.

Did this book make a difference for you?
Has CompanyCommand or PlatoonLeader added value to your professional life?

Thanks,

Nate and Tony—in your service

email us at AllenandBurgess@aol.com

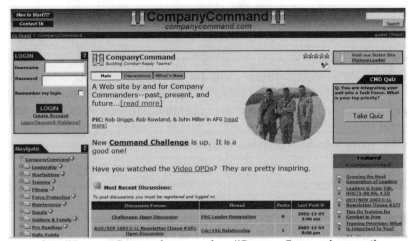

http://CompanyCommand.com ----- http://CompanyCommand.army.mil

> "CompanyCommand" & "PlatoonLeader" are your professional forums. They exist to connect company-level leaders—past, present, and future—in a conversation about building combat-ready units. Join with us, tap into the experience of others, share your knowledge, participate, make a difference, & improve the profession.

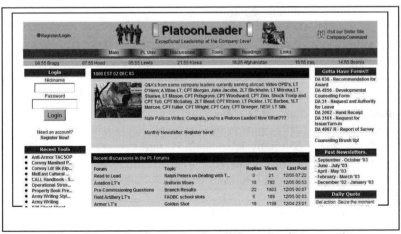

http://PlatoonLeader.org ----- http://PlatoonLeader.army.mil

Our purpose: We are on a mission to connect company commanders—past, present, and future—together in a conversation specifically about building effective units. Why? Professionals who are fiercely resolved to prepare for combat and who continually share what they are learning with each other will be more effective and will grow more effective, combat-ready units.

Brief Overview

Register via the "**create account**" button and develop your "**dog tag**" (aka personal profile). Once you create an account, you will be able to fully participate and will also begin receiving the **Company-Level Leadership (C-LL) Newsletter.**

The site is organized based on the major areas of command—Leadership, Warfighting, Training, Fitness, Force Protection, Maintenance, Supply, and Soldiers & Families—each of these with their own sub areas or topics. For example, you will find a section for the "1st 90 Days" in the Leadership Section, a resource for "Afghanistan Commanders" in the Warfighting Section, and "Family Readiness" (FRG) in the "Soldiers & Family" topic.

In addition, there are several other featured areas on CompanyCommand that we want to highlight here:

Pro Reading. This is *the* resource for the Army when it comes to professional reading. It is something you will want to incorporate into your leader development program for sure. See what books are making a difference for company-level leaders, and contribute by sharing the things you are learning from your own reading. In addition, you will find links to professional journals and books that are available online.

Rally Points. These are sub forums for specific types of company commanders. Examples include the ADA, ARNG, EOD, HQ, MI, and SBCT Commander Rally Points.

Commanders' Log. A collection of journals in which members of the profession are capturing what they are learning in real time. Tap into their experience, get involved in a conversation with them, and consider contributing to the profession by starting your own "Cdrs' Log" journal.

Video OPDs. This is a resource designed to bring you and your leaders the experiences of your comrades in the arena. Learn from leaders involved in current combat operations, and tap into timeless messages from the likes of McCaffrey, Grange and Eversmann. Here is a screen shot from one video OPD:

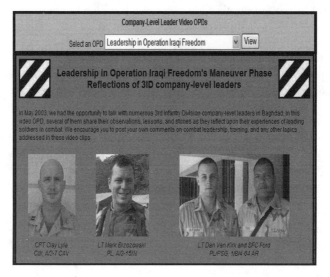

Command Challenge. This section offers you an opportunity to practice making tough leadership decisions. You will have the chance to assess a challenging situation, make choices, and join in a conversation.

We need you. Our desire is for each section of CompanyCommand to have a **"Topic Lead"** who has volunteered to give of his or her time to serve company-level leaders. Additionally, there are numerous focused initiatives our team is working, but they will only happen as members of the profession step up to the plate to contribute. **If you would like to serve your comrades in this way,** please hit the "contact us" button on the top-left side of the site and let us know. We would count it a privilege to have you on the team!

Our purpose: To serve platoon leaders who are in the arena leading soldiers and building combat-ready platoons. In this professional forum you will find a collection of shared knowledge, tools, and experiences that you can use as you lead your platoon. Moreover, you will be able to share your own ideas and experiences and participate in ongoing conversations about stuff that matters.

Current platoon leaders: Your experience is priceless. Participate not only to get the knowledge you need but also to share the knowledge you have. This is your professional forum.

Past platoon leaders: Your comrades are counting on you to share what you've learned. As current and future platoon leaders prepare their soldiers for combat, it only makes sense that they not have to reinvent the wheel.

Future platoon leaders: Join this forum and gain a real-time glimpse into what practitioners "in the arena" are learning and experiencing. Short of being there yourself, there is not a more relevant resource for you to tap into as you prepare to lead soldiers.

PL University: Where current and former platoon leaders share inspirational stories and experiences.

Discussions: This is an ongoing conversation to increase lateral communication among professionals who are dedicated to improving the practice of leadership at the platoon level.

Tools: Get ideas and save time by downloading great products, and then make a difference by sending in tools that have been invaluable to you as a platoon leader.

Readings. See what books are making a difference for platoon leaders, and contribute by sharing the things you are learning from your own reading.

Links: Contribute to or browse links to sites with valuable tools and resources dedicated to improving small unit leadership.

Bibliography

Works and Sources Cited

Associates, The Department of Behavioral Sciences and Leadership, USMA. *Leadership in Organizations.* Garden City Park, New York: Avery Publishing Group, Inc., 1988.

Amabile, Teresa. "How To Kill Creativity." *Harvard Business Review* (Sep-Oct 1998): 77-87.

Collins, James, and Jerry Porras. *Built To Last: Successful Habits of Visionary Companies.* New York: HarperBusiness, 1994.

Covey, Stephen R. *The Seven Habits of Highly Effective People.* New York: Simon and Schuster, 1989.

_____. *Principle Centered Leadership.* New York: Simon and Schuster, 1990.

Covey, Stephen R., A. Roger Merrill, and Rebecca R. Merrill. *First Things First.* New York: Simon and Schuster, 1994.

Headquarters, Department of the Army. *Field Manual (FM) 22-100, Military Leadership.* Washington D.C.: Department of the Army, 1999.

_____. *Field Manual (FM) 100-14, Risk Management.* Washington D.C.: Department of the Army, 1998.

_____. *Field Manual (FM) 25-101, Training the Force: Battle Focused Training.* Washington D.C.: Department of the Army, 1990.

_____. *Field Manual (FM) 25-100, Training the Force.* Washington D.C.: Department of the Army, 1988.

_____. *Training Circular (TC) 25-30, A Leader's Guide to Company Training Meetings.* Washington D.C.: Department of the Army, 1994.

Kouzes, James, and Barry Posner. *The Leadership Challenge.* San Francisco: Jossey-Bass Publishers, 1995.

Malone, Dandridge M. *Small Unit Leadership: A Commonsense Approach.* Novato, CA: Presidio Press, 1983.

Maxwell, John C. *Developing the Leaders Around You.* Nashville: Thomas Nelson Publishers, 1995.

_____. *The 21 Most Powerful Minutes in a Leader's Day: Revitalize Your Spirit and Empower Your Leadership.* Nashville: Thomas Nelson Publishers, 2000.

McCauley, Cynthia D., Russ S. Moxley, and Ellen Van Velsor, ed. *The Center for Creative Leadership Handbook of Leadership Development.* San Francisco: Jossey-Bass Publishers, 1998.

Meade, Dana. "Leadership." In *Leading at Mach 2* by Steve Sullivan, 183-195. New York: Edinburgh Press, 1995.

Moore, LTG Harold G., and Joseph L. Galloway. *We Were Soldiers Once... and Young.* New York: Random House, 1992.

Nanus, Burt. *Visionary Leadership: Creating a Compelling Sense of Direction for Your Organization.* San Francisco: Jossey-Bass Publishers, 1992.

Senge, Peter. "The Practice of Innovation." *Leader to Leader Journal* (Summer 1998): http://www.pfdf.org/leaderbooks/L2L/summer98/senge.html

_____. *The Fifth Discipline.* New York: Currency Doubleday, 1990.

Sullivan, Gordon R., and Michael V. Harper. *Hope Is Not A Method.* New York: Broadway Books, 1996.

Tsouras, Peter G., ed. *The Greenhill Dictionary of Military Quotations.* Pennsylvania: Stackpole Books, 2000.

Works and Sources Consulted

Ambrose, Stephen. *Band of Brothers.* New York: Simon and
Schuster, 1992.

Collins, Arthur S., Jr. *Common Sense Training: A Working Philosophy
For Leaders.* Novato, CA: Presidio Press, 1978.

Headquarters, Department of the Army. *Field Manual (FM) 22-102,
Soldier Team Development.* Washington D.C.: Department of the
Army, 1987.

Maxwell, John C. *Developing the Leader Within You.* Nashville:
Thomas Nelson Publishers, 1993.

McCall, Morgan W. Jr. *High Flyers: Developing The Next Generation
of Leaders.* Boston: Harvard Business School Press, 1998.

Meyer, John G., Jr. *Company Command: The Bottom Line.*
Alexandria, VA: Byrrd Enterprises, Inc., 1994.

Nye, Roger. *The Challenge of Command.* New Jersey: Avery
Publishing Group, Inc., 1986.

Rommel, Field Marshal Erwin. *Attacks.* Provo, Utah: Athena Press,
Inc., 1979.

Index